LANDSCAPE WITH LAKE DWELLINGS

'Oh Lord . . . who layeth the beams
of his chambers in the waters . . .'
Psalm 104

LANDSCAPE
WITH LAKE DWELLINGS
The *Crannogs* of Scotland

Ian Morrison

Senior Lecturer in Geography
University of Edinburgh

EDINBURGH
at the University Press

© Ian Morrison 1985
Edinburgh University Press
22 George Square, Edinburgh

Printed in Great Britain by
Clark Constable Ltd, Edinburgh

British Library Cataloguing
in Publication Data
Morrison, Ian A.
Landscape with lake dwellings:
the crannogs of Scotland
1. Lake-dwellers and lake-dwellings
—Scotland
2. Scotland—Antiquities
I. Title
941.1   GN785

ISBN 0 85224 472 X
0 85224 522 X paper

Contents

Robert Munro
1835–1920

Preface

A century has now passed since Robert Munro published his classic work on *Ancient Scottish Lake Dwellings or Crannogs* (1882). In that substantial book, he set out to record in detail the excavation of sites exposed by nineteenth-century drainage operations. The aim of the present slimmer volume is rather different. Since his lifetime, crannogs have received relatively little scholarly attention. For most archaeologists, the exploits of that intrepid Edwardian the Reverend Odo Blundell (who explored crannogs using a borrowed copper helmet and lead boots) served only to emphasise the impracticality of investigating them in their watery setting. In recent years, however, the situation has changed with the advent of equipment that permits archaeologists to carry out work of professional standard under water. This has opened up the possibility of undertaking systematic studies, instead of having to rely on casual access to sites that happen to emerge if water levels are lowered during agricultural or engineering operations. Furthermore, the special conditions of preservation in the lochs mean that crannogs have much to offer to modern archaeology, with its emphasis on environmental and economic aspects of sites, and on their landscape relationships. Over the last decade momentum has been gathering, and perhaps more than at any time since the days of Munro and Blundell we are at a stage where a review of aims and approaches is appropriate. The present essay seeks to contribute towards that discussion by setting out some of the ideas and methods currently under development.

It would have been pleasant had it been possible to signal the Munro centenary with an exhaustive treatise. But instead the recent fieldwork has served mainly to strip away assumptions and preconceptions (which had often hardened since his day). We have reached an intriguing place in the enquiry, where we realise just how far we remain from definitive answers on most topics related to crannogs. The small scale of the book is therefore deliberate. It does not seek to be definitive or exhaustive. Rather, its role is to review a range of avenues that invite exploration.

In 1886, just four years after Munro's *Ancient Scottish Lake Dwellings,* Lt-Col. Wood-Martin produced *The Lake Dwellings of Ireland,* a work of equivalent scope and value. There too it has long been clear that such sites are numerous, and cover a wide geographical and chronological range. Something of a renaissance of crannog studies is now also evident in Ireland, though diving techniques have as yet been used rather less than in Scotland. There are interesting divergences as well as parallels between the Scottish and Irish material. These can not be treated adequately in an essay of the present scale. Though this book therefore focuses on the Scottish material, it is hoped that it will help to further more widely based discussions in the future, not only with our Irish colleagues but with others elsewhere who are also interested in wetlands and small island settlements.

After a discussion of the nature of the crannogs and of their setting in Part One of the book, Part Two considers technical aspects of surveying and excavating in lochs. The recent activity in Scotland owes much to the experience of Europeans and Americans involved in the development of methods for carrying out serious archaeological work on sites lying in water. One of the aims of Part Two is to offer something in return to those already engaged in underwater work, who have been generous with their own technical information. The other aim is to indicate the problems and possibilities to any 'dry-land' archaeologists who may succumb to the lure of the crannogs, and contemplate participating in this type of amphibious investigation.

A quarter of a century of fieldwork in various parts of the world has left the writer in no doubt that on a good day the Scottish lochs can be amongst the most beautiful and satisfying of places to be. Not all days are good ones however, and the pursuit of the crannog has its measure of mud, misery and midges. Working in water is frequently uncomfortable and sometimes dangerous, and one soon finds who are the ones to ride the river with. The writer is grateful for the good fellowship down the years of those durable souls, male and female.

Especial thanks are due to Dr and Mrs Duncan McArdle, and to Dr Nicholas Dixon. The participation of the McArdles was intrinsic to the success of the Loch Awe project. The technical breakthrough of the Loch Tay excavation, and much else, reflects the initiative of Nick

Dixon. Whilst they must be exonerated from responsibility for the book's shortcomings, the writer is happy to acknowledge that its positive aspects owe much to their shared liking for innovative field-work, and for argument spiced with pawkie Scots humour.

Notes

ILLUSTRATIONS. Many of the sites discussed lie underwater, and few readers are likely to be divers. Illustrations thus have a special role in this essay. Where these are interpretative, source references and in some cases alternative visualisations are provided. To bring out three-dimensional relationships within sites and in the lochs and landscapes, perspective reconstructions and block diagrams have been created. To secure geometrical consistency in these, use was made of a Forster (Schaffhausen) Perspektomat P-40, and of an Apple microcomputer linked to a digitiser and Robotics Bitstik interactive graphics system. To aid comparisons, plans and axonometric views have been presented as far as possible at common scales. Except where noted otherwise, drawings are by the author, as are the surface and underwater photo-graphs in plates 2, 3, 7, 10, 14, 15, 16, 17, 20, 21, 22, 23 and 24. Mar-ginal references to illustrations are in roman type for figures, italic for plates. The illustration on page i shows an ash plaque from Lochlee crannog.

DIMENSIONS. Dimensions given in the older literature often appear to be based only on rough measurements, or indeed 'eye-ball' esti-mates. Histograms show groupings at round numbers such as fives and tens, so when a feature was reported as '45 feet' or '15 yards' across, this probably means no more than that it looked over forty but less than fifty feet wide. It would introduce a spurious impression of precision to metricate that as '13.72 m'. Dimensions are therefore quoted as originally given, with metric approximations in parentheses: '45 feet (c. 14 m)'. Where metres alone are given, this indicates modern measurements actually taken on the metric system.

DATES. In accordance with convention, dates stated in uncalibrated radiocarbon 'years' have been distinguished by lower case (bc) from calendar dates shown in capitals (BC, AD). These 'raw' radiocarbon determinations are calculated on the 5568-year half-life.

Acknowledgements

The genesis of this essay was an invitation from the Munro Lectureship Committee, University of Edinburgh, to organise a symposium on crannogs on the occasion of the centenary of publication of Munro's *Lake Dwellings*. To the Committee, and particularly to Dr David Ridgway, I offer my thanks; as also to the Press Committee and staff of Edinburgh University Press for their encouragement and support.

The especial contributions of Dr and Mrs McArdle, and Dr Nick Dixon, are noted with gratitude in the Preface. It is also pleasant to recall the lively and productive days spent on Highland lochs with Professor Harold Edgerton and Mr John Mills, obtaining sonar images such as those in plates 18 and 19.

The publishers are grateful to the following for permission to reproduce illustrations: the Ordnance Survey (plate 1, Crown copyright); the National Monuments Record of Scotland (plate 13); Michael Brooks and Nick Dixon (plates 4, 5, 6, 8, 9); Batsford Ltd and Longmans Group Ltd (figure 2.2); the editor of the Proceedings of the Society of Antiquaries of Scotland (figures 2.2, 3.16; plates 11, 12); the Trustees of the National Library (figure 3.1).

Further material, not reproduced directly here, also provided visual references for the development of some of my drawings, and I am pleased to acknowledge the helpfulness of publications by the following (these are cited in the bibliography): Bocquet; Dixon; Grant; Hanson and Maxwell; Hardy; Hayes-McCoy; Ivens; Jankuhn; McArdle; Miller; Monteith; Perini; C. M. Piggott; J. Ritchie; RCAHMS; Schmid; Stewart; Williams.

The constructive (and cheerful) co-operation of the staffs of the National Monuments Record and the Map Room of the National Library of Scotland not only facilitated but enlivened the drier aspects of the research.

1. Introduction

There is something seductive about the notion of building little islands as retreats from the cares of the world. They offer a degree of asylum that should please those psychoanalysts of architectural meaning who descry in us all a deep-seated yearning to regress to the sanctuary of Adam's little hut in Paradise (Rykwert 1981). Yi-fu Tuan (1979) has gone so far as to suggest that we live in *Landscapes of Fear*. He argues that what we perceive as mental and physical threats from our surroundings have conditioned most of what humans have constructed down the centuries. Current rates of mugging and housebreaking are reflected in schemes for artificial islands such as that for San Francisco Bay, which offers high-amenity high-security apartments with 'such advantages as unapproachability by water, narrow neck to mainland easily guarded, plus all round visibility' (Clay 1980, 172). If there were any realtors in the Iron Age, one can imagine them promoting crannogs in not dissimilar terms.

In Scotland, as in Ireland, the use of crannogs is not restricted to the prehistoric period but continues until the seventeenth century AD. There is thus documentary, oral and place-name evidence to supplement the testimony of archaeology in confirming that although refuge was not the only function of the islets, it was certainly an important one. This is hardly surprising in view of the way that strife, national and factional, has characterised so much of Scotland's history. The recurrent inability of central government to secure overall civil order (e.g. Smout 1969, Donaldson 1974), often put the onus on local measures of self-protection (e.g. McNeill and Nicholson 1975). Victorian antiquaries were in no doubt that crannogs were essentially retreats. The Reverend C. W. King even concluded that such refuges would have had to be assumed, had remains not been found. Writing to John Stuart (1866, 392) about Dio Cassius on the pursuit of the *Caledonii* into their marshes, he asserted that this presupposed crannogs, 'for these Celts required a *pied à terre* literally; they could not squat for

1

weeks like a flock of wild ducks upon the surface of the morasses . . .'. The image is an engaging one. But although security was clearly often the dominant element in a decision to insulate oneself or one's goods on a small islet, it was by no means the only reason. We must guard against interpreting limited archaeological data in simplistic ways. Elucidating the full range of functions of the Scottish sites is one of the more difficult problems that they present.

1.1   People who have found reasons for building up their own islets are scattered round the world from Holland to Australasia; from lowlands in Mesopotamia and atolls in the Pacific, to as far above sea level as Lake Titicaca. In world perspective, Scotland has one of the largest concentrations of built-up island sites known. It might be argued that this is hardly surprising in view of the sheer amount of standing water in the Scottish landscape. A bathymetrical survey measured almost six hundred freshwater lochs, totalling over 880 sq. km in area (Murray and Pullar 1910). Many others, smaller or less accessible, were omitted. William Roy's military survey of mainland Scotland, made in the aftermath of the 1745 Rising, shows how the landscape was formerly even more thickly littered with lakes and ponds. This was particularly so on the better land outside the Highlands, before the extensive drainage work of the late eighteenth- and nineteenth-century agricultural improvements. The severity and relative recency of the glaciation of Scotland accounts for this contrast to much of southern Britain. There were still substantial valley glaciers pushing into the Scottish Lowlands not long before 8000 bc. Through the preceding millennia, both erosion and deposition by the ice tended to create landscapes of disrupted drainage. Basins were excavated in the bedrock, at all scales from Lochs Ness, Awe or Tay down to what Professor Walton called 'knock and lochan' (hillock and tarn) terrain. Millions of tons of boulder clay and fluvioglacial gravels choked valleys or were spread unevenly across plains, creating ponds and bogs. These offered endless scope for crannog builders.

Scope and necessity are not synonymous, however. There are many parts of the world with similarly lake-strewn landscapes where no tradition of island building is apparent. Certainly, some regions*could

Figure 1.1. Variations on the artificial islet theme: A) *Terp* or *Weirde,* Netherlands to Denmark, mainly Iron Age/Medieval; B) *Sulu Vou,* Melanesia, 20th c.; c) *S. Iraq,* marsh village, prehistoric to present day.

2

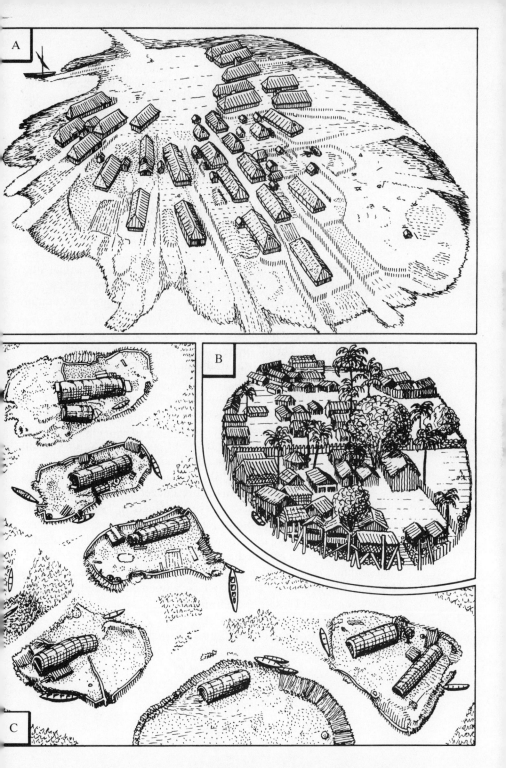

scarcely be effectively occupied at all, without recourse to island-con-
struction (viz. the Marsh Arabs of Iraq; Salim 1962, Thesiger 1964,
Young and Wheeler 1977). But in Scotland, while there are bogs and
lochs a-plenty, there is equally no shortage of firm ground. The large
number of sites can therefore hardly be said to reflect a necessity
imposed by the physical environment. Instead, their ubiquity appears
to arise from persistent traits in the local 'cultural environment'.

As more information becomes available on the contrasts and simi-
larities between Ireland and Scotland, it will be interesting to compare
the interplay of human and physical factors in each place, particularly
with respect to the concept of Atlantic Britain. The apparent scarcity
of crannogs in the Lake District, so close to Scotland and so similar in
landscape to areas of Scotland where crannogs abound, seems anomalous and surely merits field investigation. In Wales, occasional sites
akin to crannogs have long been suspected (e.g. Munro 1882), and
they are not unknown further south in England, where for example
one has recently been reported from the Fenland (Pryor 1983).

In Scotland itself, crannogs do not only figure in academic literature.
They seem to have caught the popular imagination from early times,
some being attributed by oral tradition to the famous or infamous.
King Alexander I was credited with building two dozen in Loch Tay;
Macbeth was said to have been slain on his island stronghold in *Lochan
Lùnn dà Bhrà*; while lesser murderers and reivers such as *An Stalcair
Rioch* (The Brindled Stalker) and *Ailean na Leine Ruaidhe* (Allan
Red Sark) had others as their lairs. Some were the dens of eldricht
craturs such as *Brunaidh an Eilein* (the Island Brownie) in Loch Tay,
and the Kelpie of Loch Pityoulish. In popular imagination Kelpies
guarded Loch Bruaich, even into the present century. This Loch lies in
rough country a thousand feet above sea level. In 1909, when Odo
Blundell contrived to get his half-ton of diving gear up there by horse
and cart, thunder broke out. He was warned that this marked the dis-
pleasure of the water gods at the intrusion of a copper-helmeted priest.
That crannog is also remembered as the refuge of doomed lovers, a
Highland Montague and Capulet whose elopement caused a clan battle between Lovat Frasers and Chisholms.

THE DEVELOPMENT OF RESEARCH. Serious antiquarian interest in
Scottish crannogs began to develop in the eighteenth century as sites

4

were revealed by the drainage works of the agricultural improvers, but it was in the mid-nineteenth century that archaeological momentum built up. To expanding drainage programmes was added the stimulus of vivid reports of finds of prehistoric habitation sites submerged in Alpine lakes. These started with exceptionally low water levels there in 1853–54. By 1866, Ferdinand Keller's *The Lake Dwellings of Switzerland and other parts of Europe* was available in English, complete with a *Notice of the Scotch Crannogs* by John Stuart. He was one of three Victorians to whom later students of Scottish crannogs owe much, for he laid a foundation for systematic study by collating and publishing material that would otherwise have been lost (1864–66). The others were Munro and Blundell.

Robert Munro was not afflicted by what the Swiss call *Pfahlbauromantik*; that antiquarian romance with the notion of pile-dwellings, which long persisted to hamper Continental research (Ruoff 1981). Dr Munro came with the analytical turn of mind, and training in observation, of a medical practitioner. He was eventually able to devote himself full-time to archaeological research. His *Ancient Scottish Lake Dwellings or Crannogs* (1882) remains an indispensable account not only of sites he shared in excavating, but of much else that would have passed unrecorded. Its success led to an invitation to give a lecture series to the Society of Antiquaries of Scotland, on Lake Dwellings of Europe. His response was to set out to view, at first hand, sites and museum material throughout Europe. He spent two years travelling, questioning and noting, with his wife helping with the drawings. Interpretations have of course changed, but the book that resulted (1890) is still valued internationally for the basic information it preserves. Though aspects of his work inevitably fall short of modern standards, his analytical thinking in the field, his thorough museum work, copious publications, and European rather than parochial perspective, all merit him a place as a forerunner of twentieth-century archaeology rather than as a relic of earlier antiquarianism.

Father Odo Blundell was also an innovator who believed in seeing for himself. Whereas Munro worked principally (though not exclusively, e.g.1893) in the south-west of Scotland, Blundell's interests lay mainly in the Highlands (e.g. 1909–10, 1912–13). There he not only co-ordinated the gathering of information but, borrowing gear from the Caledonian Canal divers, himself descended to observe the underwater parts of a number of crannogs, such as *Eilean Muireach* (Cherry Island) in Loch Ness (1908–9). Forty years before, the Reverend R. J. Mapleton had employed professional divers to explore the crannog in Loch Kielziebar (*Collie Bharr*) near the Crinan Canal (1870), but Blundell was amongst the very first archaeologists in Britain to use diving techniques in person.

When the First World War broke out, Munro and Blundell were collaborating in the organisation of a major crannog excavation at Loch Kinellan. Blundell joined the Fleet as a Naval padre and, because of the ageing Munro's ill health, the responsibility for the difficult dig fell upon local amateurs (Fraser 1917). Momentum was lost, and the inter-war era saw little activity except two partial excavations. One, at Coatbridge, had to be abandoned prematurely when the municipal authority refilled the loch (Monteith 1937). The other was of a crannog exposed in *Eadarloch*, part of Loch Treig. Here Professor James Ritchie's dig attracted little attention, perhaps because it was published in the midst of World War II (1942). Furthermore, the recorded use of the site was post-medieval, so it was of scant interest to prehistorians; and archaeological approaches to the historical period were not then in vogue.

11

No immediate revival of crannog studies took place after the War. So many decades with so little fresh data gave little incentive for systematic re-assessment of the information inherited from the early workers. Simplistic impressions seem to have developed: that crannogs were relatively few in number, occurred mostly in the south-west, and dated mainly from the Roman and Dark Age eras. These premises reflected the dominance of Munro's book as a source, with its bias towards sites that chanced to be drained within range of his medical practice.

The first real landmark in crannog studies since Edwardian times was the excavation in 1953 of one of two crannogs exposed in Milton Loch, Kirkcudbrightshire (C. M. Piggott 1952–53). This remains a valuable contribution, though the coincidence of the site being in the south-west, and resembling those accorded most attention by Munro, tended to reinforce the stereotype image of the Scottish crannog. So did finds there of artifacts of the second century AD. Though these show that the site was in use while the Romans were in Scotland, it is now clear from radiocarbon dates (discussed below) that the islet was

1, 12, 1.2

Figure 1.2 >

Plate 1. Milton Loch, Kirkcudbright. See figure 1.2 for location of crannogs.
(Crown Copyright reserved.)

Many crannogs now appear on the surface only as anonymous mounds, some (plate 2, above) supporting trees but others (plate 3, below) only rushes, or an angler's marker pole. Examples in Loch Awe.

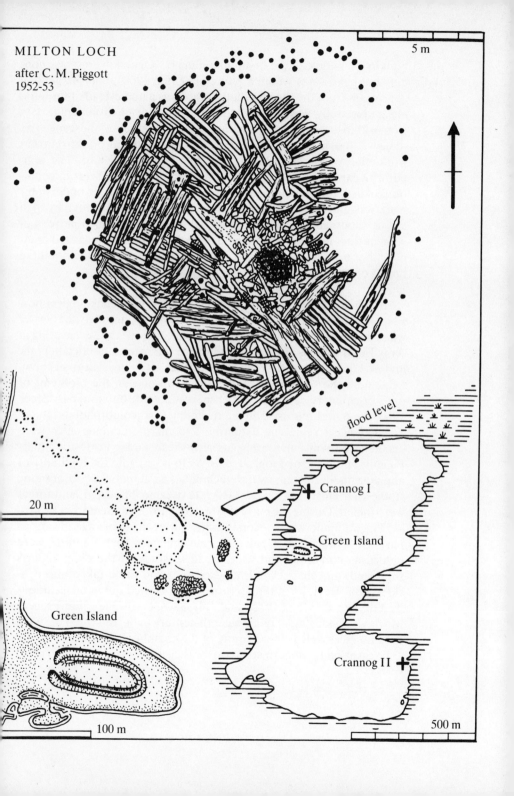

MILTON LOCH
after C. M. Piggott
1952-53

5 m

flood level

Crannog I

Green Island

Crannog II

20 m

Green Island

100 m

500 m

built in the middle of the first millennium bc. One of the radiocarbon-
4.4 dated objects was a wooden plough (Fenton 1968), and the general
conclusion from the dig was that the site was a homestead of farmers.
No major study was, however, made either of environmental data
from within the site, or of the nature of the surrounding landscape. The
same was true in the case of the only other post-war dig prior to current
work, that of the crannog in Loch Glashan, Argyllshire. The tem-
porarily-exposed top of this was investigated by J. G. Scott in conditions of difficulty, when it was partially drained in 1960. No underwater
work was undertaken either there or in Milton Loch, though by then
the development of the aqualung had made diving much more convenient than in the days of Blundell. A few sport divers visited crannogs, but to most they offered neither the glamour nor the potential
profits of wrecks.

MODERN UNDERWATER INVESTIGATION. The archaeological possibilities of diving on crannogs first became apparent to the writer
when he examined sites with the late Eric Cregeen while excavating in
Argyll in the 1960s. Eric was a sensitive interpreter of documentary
and oral as well as archaeological evidence. It is pleasant to acknowledge here the stimulus of discussions with him on the problems of
inter-disciplinary research, which pervade work on crannogs. Since
1960, the writer has used diving techniques in geomorphological and
archaeological research. Estuarine and marine crannog sites were
encountered while preparing his PhD thesis under Professor Stuart
Piggott, and it seemed logical to go on to investigate the feasibility of
applying modern underwater techniques systematically to crannog
studies. Dr and Mrs Duncan McArdle became interested, and forces
were joined. During the early 1970s, with encouragement from Professor Piggott, underwater reconnaissances were made of lochs in various
parts of Scotland. It rapidly became apparent that crannogs were
1.3 indeed as numerous and widespread as study of the older reports
suggested, and that several hundred sites had to be taken into consideration. Reviews of the literature were carried out in dissertations
by Gwynne Oakley (1973) and Lily Savory (1973), while Frances
Murray's reassessment of nineteenth-century finds confirmed the wide
date-range as well as the ubiquity of the crannogs.
Excavation to modern standards was clearly desirable, but so great

8

were the gaps in basic information on the distribution and nature of the sites that a programme of field survey seemed a necessary prelude to digging. The writer felt that, to avoid dissipating limited resources in piecemeal studies, the best long-term research design would be to operate on a modular plan, with loch basins as the unit. A systematic basis for later comparative studies could be laid by making case studies of characteristic types of basins, surveying their natural and archaeological features from lakebed to watershed. For reasons discussed below, Loch Awe and Loch Tay are amongst the most interesting of the larger Scottish lochs. In 1973, he therefore approached Naval Air Command S.A.C. for facilities, and by courtesy of their Flag Officer set up an archaeological and geomorphological survey of Loch Awe. He invited the McArdles to join him, and the survey was carried through as a joint project between teams of divers from the Royal Navy and Edinburgh University.

1.4

Dr Ulrich Ruoff of Zurich, who has directed much of the leading modern work on the submerged settlements of Switzerland, then visited the writer while they were collaborating on an atlas of the world's submerged sites (Muckleroy ed. 1980). For comparative purposes, he wished to dive on Scottish sites. Along with T. N. Dixon, they inspected crannogs in both Loch Awe and Loch Tay during 1979. The standard of preservation of organic material in these Highland lochs appeared as good to Dr Ruoff as in the Alpine lakes. However, he confirmed that the crannogs were indeed very different from the submerged lake-side settlements with which he was familiar in Switzerland and France. He encouraged further work, and was generous with his experience in developing techniques for high standards of excavation underwater.

In 1980 Nicholas Dixon began an experimental excavation of Oakbank crannog in Loch Tay, having first completed a survey of that loch as a whole, to complement the Loch Awe study and to provide a context for the excavation. The survey and excavation together formed the basis of his PH D work under Professor Denis Harding and the writer. Despite the long history of archacological interest in the crannogs of Scotland, Oakbank is the first case where a controlled excavation has been carried out underwater by using diving techniques.

10

Because of the variety and wide date-range of crannogs, no single site is going to answer more than a small proportion of the questions

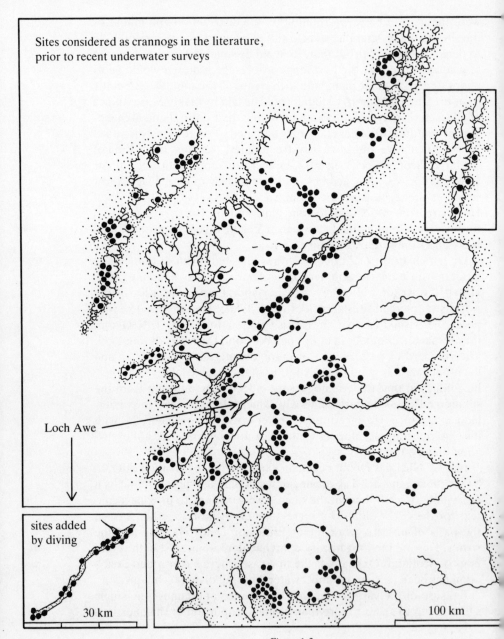

Sites considered as crannogs in the literature,
prior to recent underwater surveys

Loch Awe

sites added
by diving

30 km

100 km

Figure 1.3

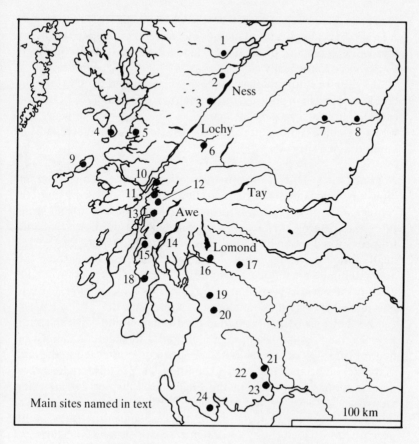

1	Loch Kinellan	13	Loch a'Phearsain
2	L. Bruaich	14	L. Glashan
3	Cherry Island	15	L. Kielziebar
4	L. nam Ban Mora (Eigg)	16	Dumbuck
5	L. nan Eala	17	Coatbridge
6	Eadarloch	18	Lochan Dughaill
7	L. Kinord	19	Buston
8	Banchory	20	Lochlee
9	L. nan Cinneachan (Coll)	21	Friars Carse
10	Eriska	22	Milton Loch
11	Lochavoullin	23	L. Arthur (Lotus)
12	L. Nell	24	Dowalton

Figure 1.4

11

they pose. In one sense, therefore, the Oakbank dig is of limited value. It is, however, important in methodological terms. By demonstrating that work to modern professional standards can be carried out effectively and economically on crannogs that have *not* been drained, it allows sites for future intensive investigation to be selected in terms of considered research policies, rather than according to the exigencies of casual drainage. This perhaps marks the most important advance that we may claim a century after Munro's classic book summarising Scotland's drained sites.

REFLECTIONS. Distaste for the discomfort and problems of amphibious operations may not be the only factor that delayed twentieth-century work on crannogs. In professional archaeology, career structures and patterns of research were long characterised by a tendency towards specialisation by period. The use of built-up islets does not fall neatly into a particular Montelian era, for their use spans some two and a half millennia at least. Nor does their map distribution readily identify them with a particular culture, in the Childean sense. Current museum labels may state that '. . . it is noteworthy that all those which can be shown to be not later than the Roman period occur in south-west Scotland', and revisions of major books still maintain that 'Crannogs of Iron Age or Roman date are apparently restricted to the land of the Novantae and Damnonii' (Cunliffe 1978, 228). But radiocarbon determinations from sites in the Highlands (chapter 2) show that views such as these are now untenable. With so many crannogs as yet undated, and many of the islets in any case appearing to be multi-period sites, it is not easy to design research strategies in terms of narrow period-specialisation. Typological dating by simple inspection is not reliable. The exterior forms of crannog mounds generally reflect the exigencies of building at the desired locations, rather than their date. Even neighbouring sites that can be shown to be contemporary can be quite different in aspect, while others of widely differing date may look alike. To be able to identify sites as being of the same period, a large programme of radiocarbon or dendrochronological work would thus be necessary. As Milton Loch shows, in many cases excavation would be required to clarify whether the initial construction of the crannog might not belong to another era altogether from the material accessible in upper layers. Furthermore, in both prehistoric and historic times the dominant impression is that the islets were a specialised but integral part of the system of life in the landscape as a whole. There is little to support the existence of a separate culture-group of *krannogervolk*.

Happily, crannogs appear to fit more readily into emerging patterns of archaeological research than into the traditional frameworks. Multi-period sites are now more often regarded as advantageous than embarrassing; and with environmental and economic research well established, landscape studies and exploitation of the special potential of wetlands sites have both acquired considerable momentum. It would therefore seem an appropriate time to seek to resuscitate crannog studies.

Much of the archaeological activity in wetlands now apparent world-wide (e.g. Muckleroy ed. 1980, Coles 1984) reflects contributions made by Alpine workers towards establishing the scientific potential of lake sites (Ruoff 1981). Progress in the Alps can hardly be said to have proceeded serenely since the nineteenth-century discoveries, however. As Joos put it (1982, 44), Emil Vogt 'celebrated the [1954] centenary of lake-dwellings by denying their very existence . . .', dismissing over-water pile dwellings in favour of lake-side land settle-   1.5
ments preserved by inundation. Since then, re-interpretations and further excavations of Swiss, French and Italian sites have created wide acceptance that around the Alpine lakes 'one has to take every possibility into consideration . . .' (Pauli 1984, 71; cf. Ruoff 1981, Strahm 1976, Perini 1976, *inter al.*). Lake-level changes there have left a varied legacy of sites preserved by waterlogging or full submergence. These run the gamut from what were originally solid-ground shore-settlements, *via* some with provision for damp and unstable subsoil to others built to cope with occasional flooding, before reaching true lake-dwellings perched on tall piles over perennial water. Though represented, these last have not proved to be the general rule, as was assumed for so long. The era of the *Pfahlbauromantik* has passed.

In Scotland, re-assessments have not so far proved so traumatic. It is clear that there are several distinct categories of sites preserved in Scottish waters (chapter 2); but it still seems acceptable that the sites generally referred to by archaeologists as *crannogs* were deliberately built up with the intention that they should be used as islands. No Scottish or Irish Vogt rose to deny this at the symposium held in Edinburgh

13

in 1982 to mark the centenary of Munro's book. As noted above, Dr Ruoff confirmed by first-hand underwater observation that sites such as those in Milton Loch, Loch Awe and Loch Tay differ fundamentally from the flooded lake-side settlements of Alpine waters. Radiocarbon dates show that several of the Scottish sites he inspected are prehistoric. For later times, documents and oral traditions in both Scotland and Ireland yield many examples of people using islets which either the testimony itself or field inspection confirm to be built-up. Since both the historical and the archaeological evidence corroborates that deliberate island-raising took place, the basic nature of Scottish lake sites has thus proved less contentious than that of the Alpine ones. It is ironic that the very absence of controversy has probably contributed to the disparate amount of research in the two areas. In terms of the standards of present-day archaeology, much less is known of crannogs than of the more obviously problematic continental sites.

Crannogs are in fact rather paradoxical antiquities, in several respects. In terms of Scottish archaeology, they are amongst the most persistently used types of site, and amongst the most ubiquitous; and they are characterised by remarkable preservation of organic materials (including artifacts and structures of types ordinarily lost on dryland sites, as well as environmental data). Yet, because of that watery setting which secures the quality of their remains, they are amongst the least studied, relative to their potential for yielding information. There is scope for fresh research on their chronology, distribution, numbers, form and construction, together with their functions and relationships within the physical and human landscapes in which they lie. To a great extent, they have hitherto been invisible antiquities, out of sight and out of mind in the cold, peat-dark lochs to which they owe their survival.

Figure 1.5. Explorers' pictures, such as A) *Papuan Gulf,* 1821, influenced early interpretation of Alpine sites as over-water 'pile dwellings', as popularised in B) Keller, *Lake Dwellings of Switzerland,* 1866. It is now recognised that these sites represent a range of relationships to changing lake levels (C). Many not underwater were in fact originally lake-*side* settlements (D).

14

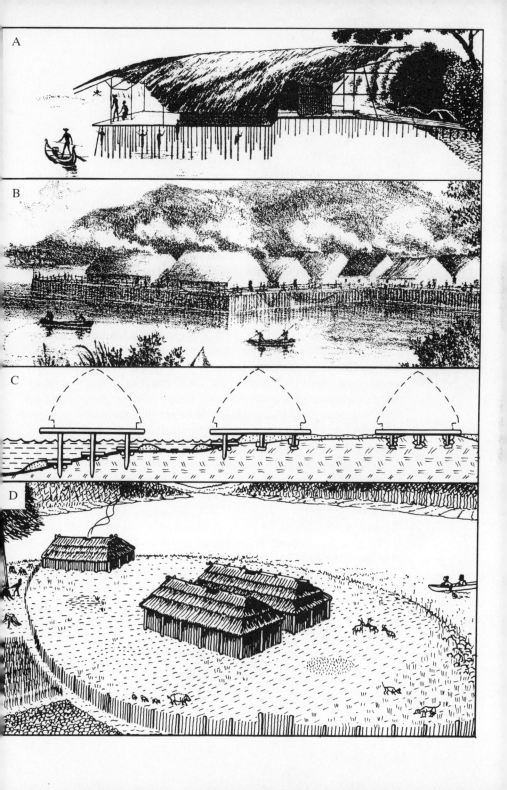

2. On Definition

At first glance, there would seem to be no great difficulty in defining a crannog. To many, the word conjures up a lake dwelling, with a round hut set upon an artificial island. This image owes much to Munro, and has been reinforced by the Milton Loch dig. A reconstruction based on the latter appears as a persuasive model in the much-visited main museum of Glasgow, and has been reproduced as drawings in newspapers, children's books and posters, as well as more academic publi-

2.1 cations, for thirty years. It has probably been as influential on the popular impression of Scottish crannogs as that prime tourist attraction, the full-size Craggaunowen replica, has become of Irish ones.

2.2 However, our renewed awareness of the sheer number of sites makes it appear unwise to accept too readily an image so sharply focused on interpretations of a limited range of prototypes, none of which was totally excavated. One cannot but recall the way that the vivid but premature nineteenth-century conception of pile-dwellings long hampered research in the Alpine lakes. It would thus seem best to regard the definition of crannogs as an objective rather than a precursor of research. Let us therefore review problems that have to be taken into account before a definitive characterisation may be evolved.

BASIC CRITERIA. Just as in the Alpine province it is now evident that there is a continuum from accidentally submerged lake-side sites through to intentionally water-surrounded settlements, so too in Scotland a wide spectrum of wetland, estuarine and lacustrine sites seems in principle likely. That they indeed occurred can readily be confirmed from reports of the eighteenth- and nineteenth-century agricultural drainage phases (for example in the *Statistical Account* of the 1790s, and the *New Statistical Account* of the 1840s). These and more recent casual finds, indexed in the National Monuments Record, make it clear that the old wetlands were rich in antiquities. From Dumfries-shire to Aberdeenshire, there are intriguing reports of 'castles' in bogs,

16

some apparently of wooden construction. Such early descriptions are however tantalisingly brief, and all too often the sites were destroyed by the operations that brought them to notice. Other sites that have been described as crannogs were found in rivers, estuaries and sea firths, from Marchburn in the south-west *via* the Clyde and Eriska (off Lismore), to the Beauly Firth in the north. Though they vary considerably in form and possible function, several of these non-lake sites are certainly deliberately built-up islets, and some will be considered below.

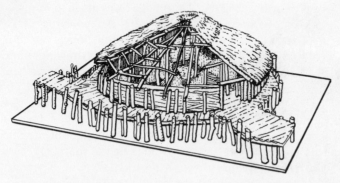

Figure 2.1. Model of *Milton Loch* crannog by J. & M. Scott, in Glasgow Art Gallery & Museum.

By no means all the artificial mounds in tidal and river waters are relevant, however. Geologically out-of-place stones may be dumped ballast, or indeed the site of an abandoned vessel. We owe much of our knowledge of early ships to the effectiveness of ballast mounds in protecting their wooden structures, so one should not cry crannog on finding ancient worked timbers under stone heaps. Equally, there is much of archaeological interest in inland lochs besides crannogs. Loch Eye in Easter Ross, for instance, contains a substantial number of shallowly submerged circles of stones. Inspecting them underwater, the writer confirmed they were simply-built, but certainly artificial. They do not otherwise resemble any known crannog site, however, and were perhaps flax-retting pounds (Morrison 1978a ; *Acta Parl. Jacobi VI* 1606 *cap.*12 IV 287). Again, when sonar surveys disclosed other circular stone features on the bed of Loch Ness, a submerged village site *19* was suggested. A combination of diving and documentary research,

17

B

A

C

D

E

F

however, allowed the writer to establish that their relevance was in fact to industrial archaeology. They are not constructions, but spoil from the *Prince Regent,* one of the world's earliest steam dredgers, developed there by Telford during the Napoleonic Wars, to help link the loch into the Caledonian Canal (Morrison 1982). As these examples show, although superficial resemblances between roughly circular sites lying underwater may initially give rise to confusion, fieldwork can soon establish that some examples lie outwith any conceivable definition of a crannog.

Other cases can be more difficult to assess. Shore-side sites, like some of those now identified in Alpine lakeside wetlands, may well be represented in Scotland (one possibility is on the site of Loch Mye, near Stranraer). Much, however, remains to be learnt about variations of lake levels through time, and about the chronology of sites relative to these. It is therefore unwise to base broad generalisations on the vertical position of sites, seeking to conclude that some must always have been islands, whereas others should have been on shore for most of their duration. The situation and nature of each has to be assessed individually.

Where it can be shown that a site was used essentially as a shore establishment, however, most archaeologists would probably concur that it should not be called a crannog, even if it ultimately owed its preservation to waterlogging. This is a point on which modern and historical usage of the word apparently agrees. Central to the concept of the crannog is the idea that (though some might dry out from time to time) it was in essence a site deliberately *intended* to be utilised as an island, whether in free water or as a dry point in a swamp.

To most people, the word also implies an islet that is in some measure man-made. What this may involve is discussed further in chapter 3. For the moment, however, the implication of at least partial construction seems a useful distinction to maintain. To define a crannog simply as an artificial island is, however, misleading. Our forebears have left little sign of wishing to build *completely* artificial islands on some point of principle. On the contrary, the field evidence shows

Figure 2.2. The crannog stereotype. A) *Oakbank,* Loch Tay, a recent reconstruction (Dixon 1982); B) to E) *Milton Loch I* from, respectively, an archaeological guide, a schoolbook, a magazine article and a prehistory of Scotland; F) *Craggaunowen,* Co. Clare, Ireland, the full-size replica built in the 1970s.

19

them building as economically as possible, often augmenting natural features of the loch beds rather than going in for *ab initio* construction. One thus finds a range of degrees of artificiality. The Royal Commission distinguishes between certain classes of monuments in quantitative terms, in its naming policy. A corresponding classification might be developed, determining which sites were to be designated crannogs in terms of the percentage of their volume that was artificial. This would, however, seem unlikely to be productive for archaeological purposes, even if it were feasible to make such estimates without excavation. Documentary and field evidence alike suggest that when people wanted a small islet, they adopted, adapted or constructed one, whichever seemed most convenient. They showed flexibility in exploiting whatever nature offered in the area where they wished to locate themselves. As we shall see, of twenty sites in Loch Awe, sixteen clearly take advantage of natural features. Without digging, one cannot eliminate the possibility of a natural core inside the remainder, too.

CONSTRUCTION AND USE. Views on the actual structural techniques used by the island builders still often seem to reflect those expressed by Munro a century ago. Some procedures he envisaged (Munro 1882, 262–3) seem difficult to accept, and in any case his interpretation was based on incomplete excavation of a chronologically and geographically limited range of sites, with methods that were hardly those of modern wetlands practice. Some more recent writers, including C.M. Piggott in the Milton Loch report, have adopted his view that Lowland and Highland crannogs differ, but the fieldwork of the last decade has shown that it is simplistic to imagine a neat division into timber- and stone-construction provinces, respectively. Even non-disturbance surveys demonstrate that many stony mounds in Highland lochs contain substantial timber components, and one of the most interesting results so far from the Oakbank excavation is Dr Dixon's suggestion that some sites, which now appear as stone mounds, may originally have been built as essentially wooden structures, being reinforced with boulders only later in their lives. With possibilities such as these emerging, we are far from a definitive typological classification of the internal structure of crannogs. The range of techniques used by the islet builders is yet another area where it now seems even more

20

desirable than before to eschew preconceptions and encourage fresh research. For the moment it thus seems best to frame any definition of crannog in fairly neutral terms, perhaps calling it a 'built-up' islet, but resisting any implication that it is necessarily wholly artificial, and avoiding pre-judging the nature of the internal structure.

As to what stood on top of crannog islets, Munro was rightly cautious. Like all other investigators before and since, he was faced with the problem that though a watery environment can give outstanding preservation below the waterline, superstructure tends to rot, wash away or be broken up. Often little intelligible remains, even of stone wall footings. Due largely to the Milton Loch reconstruction, the popular image is of a circular hut. However, both in principle in terms of the date range now realised to be involved, and from field observations, this was clearly not exclusively so. As Munro recognised (e.g. 1899), rectangular structures are certainly represented as well.

Regarding the functions of the buildings, nineteenth- and twentieth-century excavations and documentary evidence alike confirm that, in both the prehistoric and historic periods, built-up island sites that functioned as true lake dwellings are widely represented in Scotland. In both the Highlands and the Lowlands, some give a very full picture of life in a farmer's steading. However, since it is equally evident there was a wide range of other uses for built-up islets (chapter 4), it is best not to use the term 'lake dwelling' too freely. Even where there is a strong case for believing that the islet played a part in the life of a farming community, it is not always clear that its main role was as a residence, rather than as a safe store for produce, say.

Consideration of possible uses re-introduces the problem of assessing just how far individual sites had security as their primary aim: and if so, whether security of persons, or for goods, livestock or harvests; and whether from two- or four-footed predators. Sometimes there may well have been a dual intention, with the labour of building up an islet seeming worthwhile because it would provide not only a vermin- and pilfer-proof store in ordinary times, but also a refuge for the family in an emergency. Function, security and nature of access are clearly related.

Movement across water involves particular constraints and opportunities. Boats of different kinds can offer considerable advantages in certain roles, but are inconvenient or downright dangerous in others.

The balance between convenience and risk in providing direct access by gangway must have been a matter of canny judgement. As yet, little systematic consideration has been given to the special relationships crannogs must have had to other sites and to their environmental and economic context, by virtue of their characteristic landscape setting.

In these aspects, and in others too, we must beware of assuming that what may be established for one period is necessarily applicable earlier or later. This problem, present throughout archaeology, is particularly acute for crannogs, because their use spreads over such a wide time span. As Lloyd Laing has put it (1975), of all the native settlement types that lasted in Scotland from prehistory through the Middle Ages and into the post-medieval period, crannogs were seemingly the most persistent of all.

CHRONOLOGY. Although it is now evident that in Scotland built-up islets must have been used over at least two and a half millennia (Morrison 1983), there are still many problems regarding their chronology. It is not even clear when they finally fell out of use. In a sense this has not yet happened, in that anglers and wildfowlers find such islets convenient bases. Their hearths, butts and jetties can complicate the interpretation of earlier structures. Other sites were augmented or modified in the eighteenth and nineteenth centuries, to ornament the prospect in front of stately homes. One in Loch Tay was refurbished for a visit by Queen Victoria. Some islands have further recreative roles of which she might scarcely have approved. As one irascible visiting academic remarked, the crannog (like that other appurtenance of the Scot, the kilt) seems ideally adapted to drunkenness and fornication. In Scotland as in Ireland there was a certain resurgence in their use post-dating the introduction of whisky duty, with independent-minded distillers valuing their seclusion. This has archaeological implications, since some rotary querns that turn up as surface finds on crannogs may have more to do with potheen than prehistory.

Aside from dodging the gauger, their last use as a refuge may have been in the aftermath of the 1745 Rising, if only as bivouac sites. In the previous century, island retreats were still considered a quite routine recourse in times of trouble, at least in the Highlands. As late as 1680 an account of Strathspey describes *Loch an Eilean* as 'useful to the country in time of troubles or wars, for the people put in their goods

4

22

Plate 4. *Spar Island,* Loch Tay: the crannog refurbished for Queen Victoria's visit.

Plate 5. *Dall Farm* crannog, Loch Tay, illustrating how submerged sites can be detected from the air.

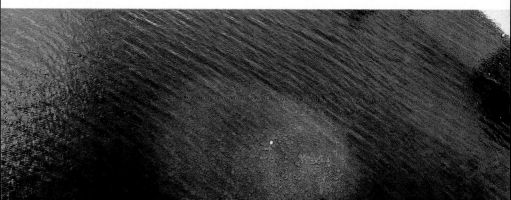

Plate 6. *Croftmartaig Island,* Loch Tay, showing how aerial photography can reveal the underwater configuration.

and children here; and it is easily defended . . .' (in Stuart 1866, 32). At the beginning of that century it is evident that, as in Ireland, crannogs were still sufficiently important militarily for central government to take note of them. For example, when there was trouble in the Western Isles, the Register of the Privy Council of Scotland records that an admonition is to be delivered

> to Angus McConeill of Dunnyvaig and Hector McClayne of Dowart [Duart] for the obedience of thame and thair clannis. 14 Aprilis 1608 . . . That the haill houssis of defence strongholdis and cranokis in the Yllis perteining to thame and their foirsaidis sal be delyverit to his Maiestie and sic as his Heynes sall appoint to ressave the same to be vsit at his Maiesty's pleasour. (*R.S.C.: Acta penes Marchiarum et Insularum Ordinem* 1608–23).

At what point in the seventeenth century crannogs lost their importance has yet to be established. As late as 1646, Campbell of Glenorchy was awarded maintenance for having garrisoned the Yle of Loch Tay with forty men and kept it for 14 months 'against the rebelle for the good of the publict' (*Acta Parl. Caroli I, cap.*89 vi). The island is at least partly artificial, and the length of occupation suggests that it was properly fitted out for inhabitation. However, it is larger than the sites commonly accepted as crannogs, and it had also lain abandoned for over eighty years before Campbell put it in a state of defence (Gillies 1938). It thus remains difficult to judge whether more typical islets were still regularly used as dwellings at so late a date. This is not inconceivable in the fastnesses of the Highlands. In a note contributed to the second edition of Keller's *Lake Dwellings,* Kinahan suggests that at least one Irish crannog was inhabited on the threshold of the nineteenth century. 3.6

The end of the period of regular occupation is thus difficult to fix. Nor is it easy to be sure when the actual building of islets other than for recreational or ornamental purposes ceased. A statement regarding the construction of one in Loch Lochy for Lord Cumming was written in the 1630s, but refers to earlier events (see chapter 3). It seems, however, that his was not the last crannog built there:

> In the year 1580, in order that he might subdue the insolence of the Lochaber men, Mackintosh caused an island in the loch, commonly called Loch Lochy, to be constructed, which was called Ellan-darrach, that is, the oaken island, for it was built upon

oaken beams . . . In that island he placed a garrison, and whilst it was there all the people of Lochaber were very submissive to their superiors, but as soon as the island was broken down they relapsed into their wonted rebellion and mischief. (*History of the Mackintoshes,* quoted in Blundell 1909–10, 27)

Lachlan Mor Mackintosh's 1580 campaign in Lochaber involved a force of 2 500 men, so it was sufficiently newsworthy to be chronicled. It is difficult to discount the possibility that other islets may have been constructed later in less dramatic circumstances, and failed to enter the historical record.

We can at least place the historical end of the crannog era in Scotland to within a century or so. This is not yet true of its prehistoric beginning, though some radiocarbon dates are now available. So far, all of these fall in the first millennium bc. Since the calibration to calendar years for that period is still open to discussion (e.g. Ottaway ed. 1983), they are given here in uncalibrated form. The oldest is 595 bc ± 55 (GU 1323), from Oakbank crannog, under excavation in Loch Tay. Other determinations from that site give later dates, which appear to accord well with this in their places in the constructional sequence (Dixon 1981, pers. comm. 1984). A nearby site off Fearnan Hotel yielded 525 bc ± 55 (GU 1322), while that off Firbush Point towards the other end of Loch Tay gave 190 bc ± 55 (GU 1324). The one off Ederline in Loch Awe registered 370 bc ± 45 (UB 2415) from a sample approximately one hundred rings into a large timber, suggesting it may have been used on the crannog around 270 bc (Morrison 1981b). The dates from Milton Loch were 400 bc ± 100 (K 1394) from the ard incorporated in the structure, and 490 bc ± 100 (K 2027) for the pile sampled underwater (Morrison 1981a).

These determinations seem satisfactory in themselves, but too much should not be read into them. Even in the case of the two excavations, they can not be proved to represent the absolutely earliest phases of the sites, and at the non-excavated sites the aim was simply to secure material that was manifestly *in situ,* while causing the minimum of disturbance. The origin of these sites may therefore predate the emplacement of the timbers accessible for dating. So far, the total number of sites sampled remains very small indeed relative to the number of built-up islets known to exist. We have no proven basis for telling by inspection which are likely to be earliest, so the choice has reflected the

24

pattern of work in progress, rather than any attempt to spot the earliest in the country. It will be surprising if this initial selection includes these, especially since most of these dates refer to impressively developed structures that hardly look like preliminary steps in the evolution of artificial islets.

It is thus not unlikely that in Scotland the islet-building tradition extends back beyond the conventional Iron Age, into at least the Late Bronze Age. It has been suggested that the development of forts and a range of other protected settlement types implies a transition to a more turbulent society than seems characteristic of the foregoing period around the end of the second millennium (A. and G. Ritchie 1981). As more dates become available, it will be interesting to see whether crannogs first emerge in significant numbers at about that time. Indeed, it is by no means inconceivable that, as in the case of the Continental and indeed Irish wetlands sites, it may eventually prove necessary to contemplate an even longer chronological perspective than this. The value of secure bases at locations where the complementary resources of contrasting habitats may be exploited has long been recognised. It seems unlikely that the possibilities of lake and marsh settlements were disregarded until late in prehistory, in a landscape so well endowed with waterbodies and peatlands as ancient Scotland.

Be that as it may, even with conservative calibration of the radiocarbon determinations, the present direct evidence bears out Laing's contention that crannogs have been one of the longest-favoured elements in the settlement pattern of Scotland. This being so, with so many questions still outstanding it is interesting to consider what insights the historical use of the word *crannog* might offer.

LINGUISTIC EVIDENCE. Unlike technical terms such as *unenclosed platform settlement,* say, which are of our own creation, *crannog* had currency amongst those who lived while such sites were in active use. The word is from a Gaelic root common to both Scotland and Ireland. As distinguished a nineteenth-century antiquary as Daniel Wilson favoured the form *crannoge,* but the ending is hard, as Lowland Scots speakers recognised when they referred to them as *cranokis.* In Scottish Gaelic the proper form is *crannag,* but it would be pedantic to insist on that when the Irish form *crannog* has become so widely accepted (Dwelly 1949, Oxford 1971), though Scots resist the substitution of *loughs* for *lochs* as their setting.

Certain insights can indeed be gained from the usage of past times, but what we have been bequeathed in documents and placenames is unfortunately not an easily interpreted legacy, from which a definition of crannog well founded in contemporary usage may readily be deduced.

The element *crann-* implies 'wood', but, as will be shown later, it is not clear whether this refers to substructure, superstructure, or outworks. Unfortunately, *crann-* is a very widely applied root, occupying several pages of Gaelic dictionaries (e.g. Dwelly 1949, 260–4). Even the specific form *crannag* was used to refer to many more things than 'a fortified island in a lake partly natural and partly artificial' (p.261). Dwelly lists a dozen other possibilities, including a boat, mast crosstrees, pulpit, hamper, churn or hollow of a shield. He notes that the word was also applied to many other kinds of wooden structures in Gaeldom. This diversity dashes any hope that one might have gained some immediate insight into the construction of crannogs by finding that the word had close links with some particularly characteristic class of wooden object.

This multiplicity of meaning can also lead to complications if one seeks to use placenames to identify crannogs. While *A'Chrannag* can certainly refer to a built-up islet (e.g. Dwelly cites one in Loch Tollie, by Poolewe), *crann-* names present many other possibilities. For example, the old farm name *Crannich* by Loch Tay indicates simply a wooded place (Ian Fraser, pers. comm.), and no islet sites are to be found offshore there. Sometimes a placename reflects transference of meaning from wood as a material to the *form* of an object customarily made of wood. Thus, though Macpherson (1878) felt that the site at *Rudha na Crannaig* on Eigg must be regarded as a crannog on the basis of the name, it is in fact a fort on a sea cliff promontory. The name probably reflects the resemblance of the rock to a pulpit, and would be best translated as Pulpit Point. The rectangular mound in the saltings of Loch Gruinart in Islay known as *A'Chrannag* is certainly artificial and seems a more reasonable candidate for classification as a crannog. An alternative view, however, is that there again it meant The Pulpit, from the Macdonald's use of the mound for giving his orders before the battle of *Traigh Gruineart* in 1598.

If not all features in the landscape with *crann-* names are necessarily what modern archaeological practice would class as crannogs, it is equally evident that many built-up islets which we would tend to call crannogs were not named as such in the period of their use. They were commonly referred to then by words simply meaning 'island', such as *Insula, Eilean, Island, Isle/Ysle/Ylle,* irrespective of how natural or unnatural they might be. This was not only a Scottish trait. Noting the paucity of Irish *crannòc* names, MacEoin draws attention to the probable inclusion of artificial islands in the entry *Inis* in Hogan's *Onomasticon Goedelicum* (covering thirteenth- to early seventeenth-century cases). He further confirms that 'the Irish nomenclature does not make a distinction between them and natural islands' (in Rynne and MacEoin 1978, 53). Thus in both Scotland and Ireland, though documentary sources offer much of potential value, fieldwork and often the use of diving techniques will be needed to ascertain just which isles mentioned in the records are in fact artificial or part-artificial. There is very seldom as clear a statement as the one discussed in the next chapter to the effect that 'My Lord Cumming . . . builded ane Illand . . . with four bigg oak Jests that were below in the water And he builded ane house thereupone . . .'.

There is thus no Royal Road to the characterisation of crannogs *via* the documentary evidence of the historical period. Because of our uncertainties regarding original usage (explored further in the next chapter) it is perhaps unfortunate that the word *crannog* has been adopted as standard by archaeologists. We may ultimately find that the convenience of using it as a portfolio term is deceptive. The creation of a range of purely descriptive modern terms, along the lines of *unenclosed platform settlement,* might seem unattractive and pedantic, but could prove a more productive approach to the classification and analysis of so many sites, spread over such a time span.

3. On Structure and Form

'There, driving many an oaken stake
Into the shallow, skilful hands
A steadfast island-dwelling make . . .'
Lt-Col. W. G. Wood-Martin, 1886

Around 1630, *Ane Discriptione of Certaine Pairts of the Highlands of Scotland* was prepared for Sir Robert Gordon 'by a native' (Mitchell ed. 1907). His passage about an artificial island in Loch Lochy is worth quoting at length here, because it illustrates both the attraction and the frustration of available written evidence. Just as sagas tell us more about Viking personalities than their ships (Morrison 1976), so too is this concerned with what was 'newsworthy', rather than with describing things familiar to the contemporary audience.

> There was of ancient one Lord in Loquhaber called My Lord Cumming being a cruell and Tyrant Superior to the Inhabitants and ancient tennants of that Countrey of Loquahber. This Lord builded ane Illand or ane house on the southeasthead of Loghloghlie with four bigg oak Jests that were below in the water And he builded ane house thereupone . . .

Nothing further is said of the more mundane characteristics of the house. He concentrates instead on what one trusts was not one of the normal adjuncts of Highland hospitality:

> . . . ane devyce at the entrance of the said house That whaire anie did goe into the house ane table did lye by the way, that when anie man did stand upon the end theroff going fordward that end wold doune and the other goe up and then the man woman or dog wold fall below in the water and perish.

> This house being finished, the Lord Cumming did call the wholl tennants and Inhabitants of the Countrey to come to him to that house, And everie one that did come into that place did perish and droune in the water.

> And it fortuned at the last that a gentleman one of the tenants,

28

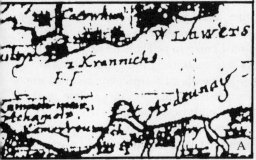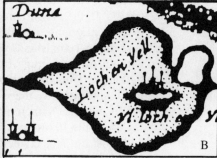

Figure 3.1. Scottish cartographic material. A) *'Krannichs'* in Loch Tay (T. Pont, *ca* 1600); B) *Loch Nell,* Lorn, symbolic treatment of site (Blaeu 1654).

who had a hound or dog in his companie, did enter the house and fall below into the water through the house, and the dog did fall efter his master. This dog being white, and comeing above the water in another place by the providence of God, without the house, the remnant tennants which were as yet on going into the house, perceiving this to be rather for their destructione and confusione . . . than for their better furtherance, did remove themselves and flitt out of that pairt wherin they were for the tyme to preserve themselves with their lives out of that cruell Mans hands.

But my Lord comeing to be advertised heirof perceiving the Countrie and tenants to be some what strong as yet, did goe away by night and his wholl Companie out of the Countrie, And never since came to Loquhaber . . .

By 1630, the ruins were underwater for most of the year:

And when summer is, certaine yeares or dayes, one of the bigg timber Jests the quantitie of an ell theroff, will be seen above the water and sundrie men of the Countrie were wont to goe and see that Jest of timber qch stands there yet, And they say that a man's finger will cast it to and fro in the water, but fourtie men cannot pull it up because it lyeth in another Jest below the water.

Neither this, nor any other early Scots or Gaelic source yet traced by the writer, offers a comprehensive contemporary description of the appearance or structure of a Scottish crannog. Scotland is also short of pictorial evidence that names sites specifically as crannogs and shows

29

them in use. Though there is some cartographic material, in Scotland (unlike Ireland) contemporary visual portrayals seem limited to high-
3.1 ly conventionalised symbols on small-scale maps. These merely indicate that certain islands we now know to be artificial were inhabited, without offering much fresh information on the actual forms of the buildings. Thus, though non-archaeological evidence can yield some intriguing insights, these are often oblique and incomplete, and to establish basic characteristics we must turn essentially to fieldwork.

Before the 1970s, measured plans were available for very few sites, and most of these lay between the Clyde and Solway. To extend this range, and to get an indication of what variability might be expected within individual loch basins, the Loch Awe and Loch Tay campaigns were mounted. To lay foundations for future comparisons within Scotland, and between Scotland and Ireland, old and new survey
3.2 material is summarised graphically here at a uniform scale, standard-
to 3.7 ising the presentation as far as available data allow. To help appreciate the three-dimensional nature of the sites, axonometric projection without vertical exaggeration is used. Some sites are shown in greater detail later. Here the aim is to provide a small-scale atlas, to give an initial impression of basic characteristics of the built-up islets, and to contribute towards their ultimate definition.

Though this is the largest corpus published so far, the selection offered here has obvious limitations. Numerically, it probably comprises less than ten per cent of the national total of such sites, and geographically the sample still omits important regions. The Loch Awe and Tay teams consider the sites located there are not untypical of others they have dived on elsewhere in Scotland. However, those lochs do not hold the full range; and within the spectrum that they do represent, their particular mix of different types should certainly not be expected everywhere.

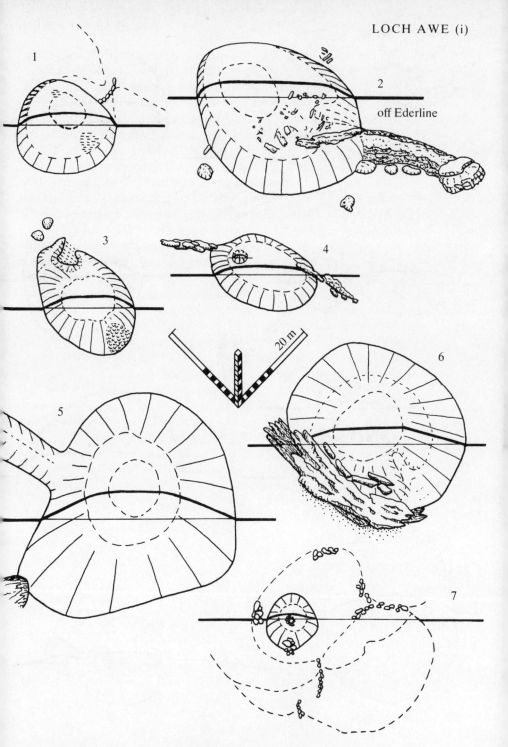

LOCH AWE (i)

off Ederline

20 m

Figure 3.2

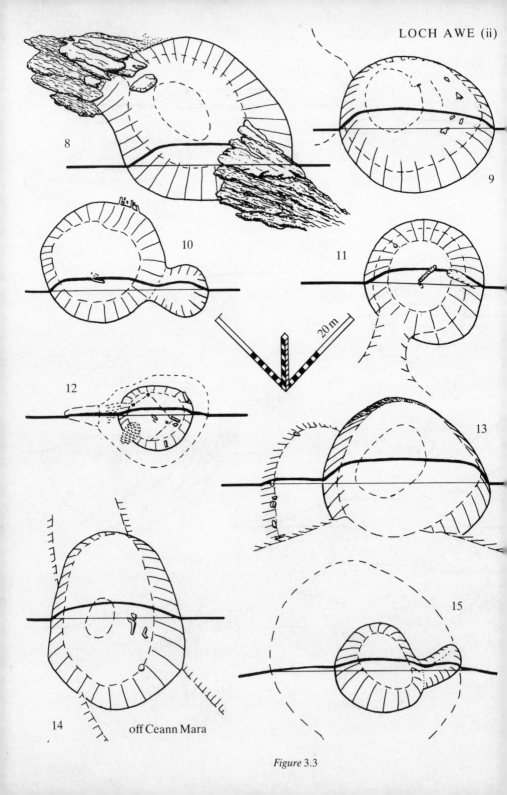

8

9

10

11

20 m

12

13

14

off Ceann Mara

15

Figure 3.3

LOCH AWE (iii)

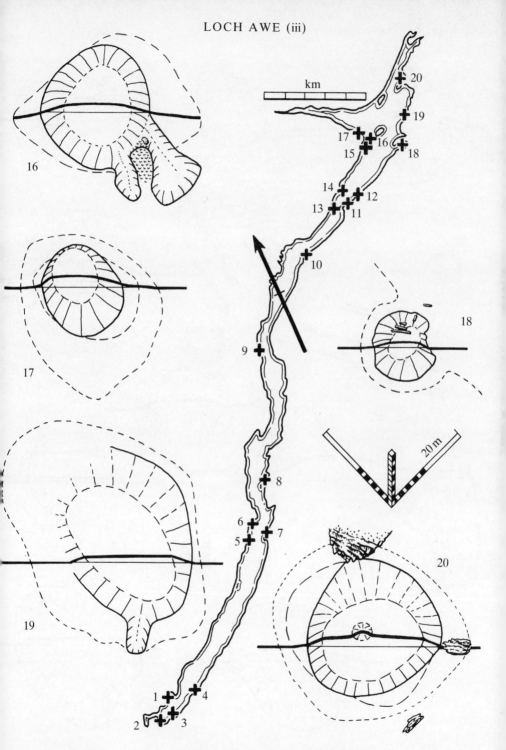

Figure 3.4

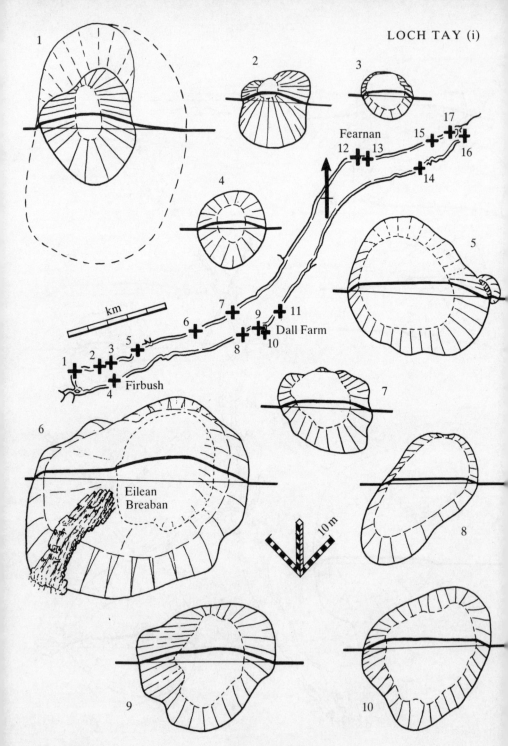

Fearnan

Dall Farm

Eilean
Breaban

Firbush

km

10 m

Figure 3.5

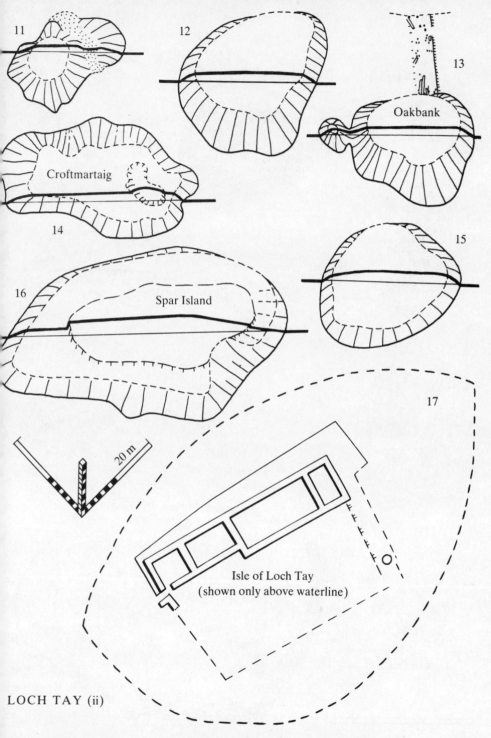

11

12

13

Oakbank

Croftmartaig

14

15

16

Spar Island

17

20 m

Isle of Loch Tay
(shown only above waterline)

LOCH TAY (ii)

Figure 3.6

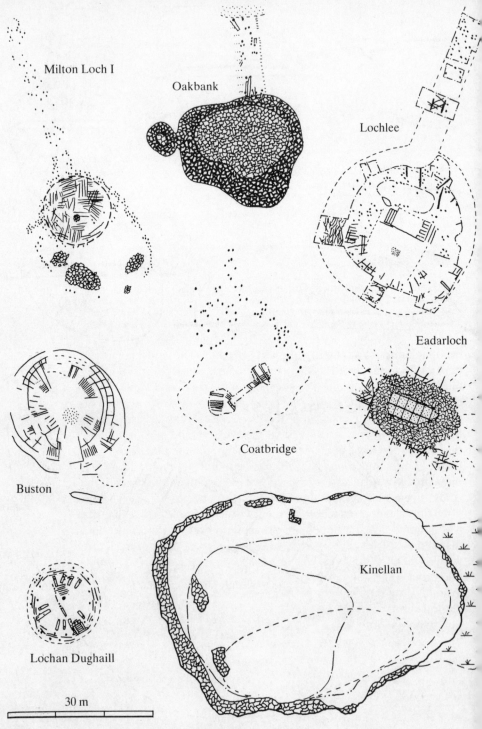

Milton Loch I

Oakbank

Lochlee

Eadarloch

Buston

Coatbridge

Lochan Dughaill

Kinellan

30 m

Figure 3.7. Size comparison of excavated sites.

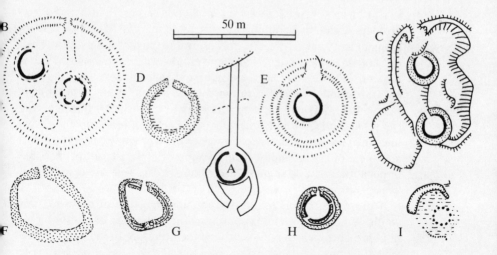

Figure 3.8. Size comparisons with small secure sites on land: A) *Milton Loch I* is reproduced for visual continuity with figures 3.2 to 3.7, which are at twice this scale; B) palisaded and C) scooped settlements; D) 'ring fort' and E) *West Plean*-style homesteads; F) *Barr Mor* and G) *Kildonan* duns; H) broch; I) souterrain.

'STONE CRANNOGS' AND 'ISLAND DUNS'. The sites portrayed here are from the Scottish Mainland and most consist of substantially built-up mounds, with the common possibility of a considerable timber component under their stony covering. New survey work, centred on the Edinburgh University field-base at Callanish on Lewis, is highlighting a problem characteristic of the Western and Northern Isles: that of distinguishing in the field between the stonier *crannogs* on rock bases, and ruinous *island duns*. It can be a difficult line to draw, and the writer is by no means convinced that it ought to be used to limit the study, since crannogs and duns overlap chronologically, and it seems often only a matter of local convenience which type of small secure site was adopted and developed. In principle, however, it is considered that dun sites are those with a notably heavy stone superstructure walling them around. Its weight usually requires a bedrock foundation, but some duns seem to be on islets that have been artificially extended, so they cannot be defined as necessarily being on fully natural bases.

37

STRUCTURAL ROLES OF TIMBER AND STONE. In discussing the problem of defining crannogs, it was noted that the idea of their islets being at least partially artificial is central to current usage of the term in Scottish archaeology. That convention will be maintained here. Recently, however, Lacy has suggested that in Donegal 'inhabited natural islands were also referred to as crannogs in earlier times' (1983, 104). Diving would be necessary to confirm that those specific islands are indeed wholly unaugmented ones, but his comment underlines the prospect that original usage of the word may have referred to an aspect of the site apart from its supporting substructure. Possible implications of this require discussion, because of the connotation 'wood', implicit in *crann-*.

If the word originally referred to superstructure or outworks this would remove the seeming contradiction in the idea of a '*stone* crannog' province, which recurs through the literature of the last hundred years. A museum label expresses it succinctly: 'there are two basic types, the crannog of stones situated in a highland loch, and the crannog built largely of piles of wood in a lowland loch or a river estuary.' This view stems largely from the experience of Munro, which was focused on sites in soft muddy environments in the Clyde and southwest. On visiting sites in different parts of Scotland, one soon becomes conscious of the close adaptation of modes of islet construction to lakebottom conditions, soft or hard, and to the potential of the landscape for supplying timber or loose rock. Regional trends are certainly apparent (e.g. stone-built island duns being commoner in the glacially scoured rocky landscape of the treeless Outer Hebrides). But within these broad trends, what was sensible and convenient for crannog builders could vary according to a much more local mosaic of constructional constraints and opportunities, with crannogs within sight of each other being built on different principles. In Loch Tay, for example, *Eilean Breaban* exploits a bedrock reef. This offered a solid raised foundation while inhibiting pile-driving, whereas others nearby are set on level sediments readily receptive of piles, though lacking the convenience of a natural mound.

8, 3.5

It is therefore too simple to think in terms of hard-edged macroregional divisions. There is in fact positive evidence, both from the old literature and from the recent diving, of the extensive use of wood in composite structures throughout much of mainland Scotland at least.

38

Plate 7. *Oakbank* crannog, Loch Tay. Underwater photograph of structural timber, showing tool marks.

Plate 8. *Eilean Breaban,* Loch Tay. Aerial view showing underwater detail.

Plate 9. *Oakbank* crannog, Loch Tay. Aerial view before excavation. It is understandable that such sites have sometimes been taken for natural mounds.

Indeed, sites apparently originally conceived as purely wooden structures have been found at points widely distributed across the so-called
'stone crannog' province of the Highlands. For example, when *Locha-
voullin* at Oban was reclaimed, Munro inspected 'a submerged platform of wooden beams laid in transverse layers . . . probing the mud,
it extended for several yards in all directions' (1890, 448). The *New
Statistical Account* reports that when a lake in the Inverness-shire
parish of Croy was drained, there was exposed not only a pile-sur-
rounded composite mound with occupation debris but also 'at about a
hundred yards distance, a circle of large piles of oak, driven deep . . .'
(xiv, 448). This may be akin to the original form of the Oakbank site
in Loch Tay, which, because of its superficial appearance, was discounted by non-diving OS field inspectors as possibly just a barren   9
mound of stones. Not only has excavation disclosed unambiguous
evidence of long-term occupation, but it suggests that the lake dwelling
may have started as a wooden pile structure, only at a later stage in its
life being encased in boulders. If this proves to be a common sequence,
it will be interesting to find whether there were synchronous phases in
which the general fashion changed from pile-dwellings *per se* to solid
mound construction. Alternatively, such a progression may have proceeded independently at individual sites, as their initial timberwork
deteriorated, and they were reinforced with rocks.

Be that as it may, the majority of recorded Scottish sites do have a   *2, 3*
stony exterior, whatever may be inside. In the case of some continental
lake sites, settlement remains were buried beneath natural deposits,
which have then been eroded differentially, to be left as stony mound
cappings (Speck 1981). On the known sites in Scottish lochs, there are
seldom any grounds for postulating that the stony covering might be
the residue of a natural deposit. This is often highly unlikely or indeed
impossible in geomorphological terms. Yet the upper surfaces of the
mounds are often sufficiently bouldery to be awkward to walk over.
Many give no impression of ever having been neatly cobbled. Indeed,
where smooth patches of small stones are encountered (as on some of
the Loch Awe sites) these attract attention, as areas that may have
been specially prepared to give better footing or to facilitate hauling
out boats (see chapter 4). Furthermore, the boulder tops of many
mounds are often awash or fully underwater for at least part of the
year. This is as true of those astride incompressible bedrock reefs as of

39

those more likely to have suffered subsidence since abandonment. The wide chronological range of the Scottish sites makes it difficult to argue that this very common submergence is due to them all dating from periods of dry climate and low lochs. In any case, it is not easy to envisage consistent water-level rises over such a range of loch basin types and regimes, Highland and Lowland, as those in which the submerged sites occur. Thus there seems a strong presumption that in many cases the surviving stony tops do not represent a surface intended for direct inhabitation, and that in some cases these bouldery surfaces may indeed always have lain below the water.

Stony mounds may thus fall into two categories:

a) Those that have substantial natural cores are unlikely to have compacted significantly during their period of use. The surviving mound may thus contain little more than the original support for a superstructure that has rotted or been eroded off the top. Where it sits on rock or other material resistant to pile-driving it may be essentially a stone-heap, unrewarding to dig.

b) Those that placed considerable reliance originally on organic materials for support would tend to have histories of subsidence, as submerged packing became waterlogged and compressed, and structural timbers rotted at the water/air interface. With continuing use, and refurbishing of superstructure, the debris of earlier stages would be pressed down into the preservative wetness beneath (to our advantage as archaeologists). Even when pinned with supplementary piles of the kind detected in the Oakbank excavation, such a mass of organic material would tend to be both unstable and vulnerable to wave erosion. It would seem reasonable to encase its sides in boulders and to spread more stones across the top, to stabilise its soft centre and give a firm substrate for fresh construction. Although anything that once rose above the last stony top has been lost, such sites would appear to offer considerable potential for the recovery not only of refuse but of elements from earlier superstructures that have settled from above to contribute to the build-up of the mound.

Angus Graham (1950–51) pointed out that early documents hint that crannogs sometimes proved cranky and awkward to build. He quotes the *Tripartite Life of St Patrick*, where it was prophesied that if Connin's descendants tried to build 'islands in a swamp (*insolas in gronna*) they would never be able to stand firmly'. Their proneness to

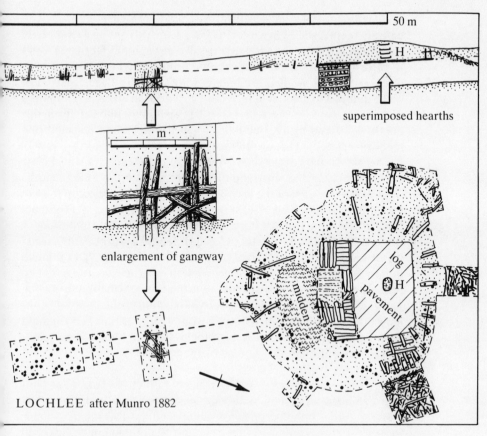

50 m

superimposed hearths

m

enlargement of gangway

log

⊕ H

pavement

midden

LOCHLEE after Munro 1882

Figure 3.9

storm damage is attested by Wood-Martin (1886), who notes that in Ireland many suffered in the great gale of AD 1477 while, according to tradition, in 990 one sank altogether in a violent tempest but was afterwards rebuilt.

In Scotland there is plenty of archaeological evidence of islets containing accumulations of organic material and occupation debris extending well below lake level. This is apparent not only at Oakbank; it is a recurrent theme in the early dig reports (e.g. Fraser 1917; Munro 1890, 1882, Stuart 1866 for summaries). One of the most vivid examples of the inundation of an occupation sequence came to light after the

41

drainage of Lochlee in Ayrshire. The artificial islet there had been entirely submerged each winter, yet was found to contain four directly superimposed hearths, spread vertically through 5·5 feet (*c*. 1.7 m) towards the top of a site that extended some 20 feet (*c*. 6 m) downward, before sterile lake sediments were reached through layers of birch and oak trunks. There were occasional artifacts, right to the bottom, where 'amongst the very last spadefuls pitched from this depth was found nearly one half of a well-formed and polished ring made of shale . . .' (Munro 1890, 410).

The lowest parts of that site extended fully 16 feet (*c*. 4.9 m) below the final level of the surrounding lake bed. Even the lower hearths were below the level of the lake deposits. The submergence of the site may thus have involved at least three processes: the internal compaction of its own materials; subsidence into the soft substratum under the increasing weight of structure and debris; and, possibly, rising water level as the small lake filled up with sediment. The relative importance of these and other factors at that particular site can not be reliably established, retrospectively, from the information in the dig report. The example, however, serves to highlight the kinds of problems that crannog users had to cope with, which we must keep in mind when interpreting what remains of their efforts to build up and maintain islets in different types of lacustrine environments.

BUILDING SKILLS AND STRUCTURAL ORGANISATION. The builders exhibited a range of skills, not least of which was the way they chose sites to economise on constructional effort. This implies sounding with staff or leadline, and presumably the probing of the lakebed to test its quality for load-bearing and pile-driving. Any determined family could shift stones, particularly if they slung the larger boulders below floats and exploited their displacement, instead of trying to lift them above the surface. But it would be interesting to know whether pile-driving was a do-it-yourself operation, or whether there was ever an element of professionalism, with specialists providing a service. *17* Some of the piles are undeniably impressive: as thick as a man's thigh, and driven deep into recalcitrant glacial clay. Special rigs are not necessarily implied. The writer has seen similar feats accomplished on the Bosphorus, by a squad of tough Turks equipped only with patience and a large boulder. Many sites give little indication of skill in carpen-

Figure 3.10 >

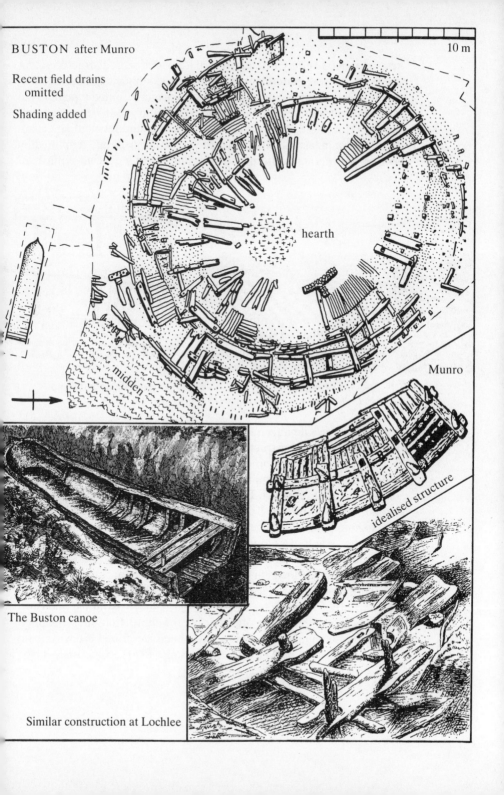

BUSTON after Munro

Recent field drains
    omitted

Shading added

10 m

hearth

midden

Munro

idealised structure

The Buston canoe

Similar construction at Lochlee

try, or indeed of any attempt to create sophisticated structures, but some do exhibit quite elegant examples of timber engineering. The use of mortice joints to interlock structures is mentioned repeatedly in reports of sites drained in the nineteenth century, but illustrations are 3.10 scarce. Munro's account of Buston (1882) is the outstanding exception, with a measured site plan that can be checked and amplified by simple photogrammetric procedures on photographs he published.

Figure 3.11. Rectangular structures. A) *Loch nan Eala* (Blundell 1911); B) *Loch Bruaich,* oak grid (Blundell 1909-10).

Buston is near Kilmaurs in Ayrshire, and many of the other reports of well-carpentered construction are also from southern Scotland, reflecting the concentration of antiquarian activity. But there are also indications that the Highlands should not be discounted. Thirty years before the visit on which Blundell was threatened by thunder and a kelpie, the islet in Loch Bruaich high above Beauly yielded a massive 3.11 rectangular grid of oak beams locked with treenails. It surrendered this to the assault of Colonel the Hon. Alastair Fraser, and though the part removed was sketched, its context was not recorded. A cross piece with pin was brought to the gamekeeper's home but 'when left to dry it crumbled to dust' (Blundell 1909–10, 14). Although this refrain and the other deficiencies of early reports are frustrating, such discoveries at least pin-point sites that seem well worth re-investigating.

Other rectangular structures have been described from time to time, for example by Mapleton at Arisaig (1870). Nevertheless, the

44

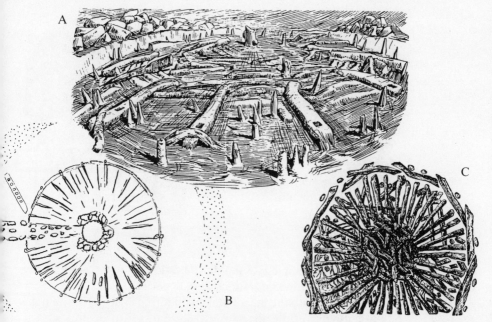

Figure 3.12. Early images of round sites with radial timbers. A) *Lochan Dughaill* (Munro 1893); B) *Dumbuck* (Munro 1905); C) *Kilmore*, Co. Cavan, Ireland (Wood-Martin 1886).

common image of a crannog site is of a round mound containing a radial pattern of timbers. Although reinforced by the Milton Loch dig, this expectation owes much to the impact of early reports of such sites in both Scotland and Ireland. Indeed, the circular concept was already   3.12 so well established a century ago that it influenced the way that some excavations were carried out, conditioning the perception of their results. Even Robert Munro was at first in danger of generating self-fulfilling prophecies. Of Lochlee, he writes (1882, 71)   3.13

we noticed . . . the tops of a few wooden piles barely projecting above the grass, which at once suggested the idea that they might be portions of a circular stockaded island. Guided by these, I completed what we supposed to be the circumference of the original island, by inserting pins of wood where the piles were deficient. Following the line thus indicated, the workmen were ordered to dig a deep trench round the mound . . . this trench ['from 5 to 6 feet

45

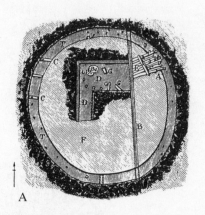

A B

Figure 3.13. *Lochlee.* The excavators' arbitrary trench (A) has
cut through structures (B).

deep'] was completed, and on the following day, 15th October
1878, systematic explorations were begun . . .

As they later found, the line of that circular trench lay well within the
actual perimeter of the site, but with its 1.5–1.8 m depth it clearly
influenced the pattern of all their future operations, and the possibilities in interpretation of the structures cut through.

In many cases radial organisation can indeed be shown to be present. However, the partly collapsed and eroded mounds that we see
today tend naturally to present a 'rounded-off' appearance, whatever
they may contain. In Loch Awe, those sites where parallel logs were
detected were not notably rectangular in outline. The danger in dis-
counting the possibility of rectangular internal structures merely from
the external impression is demonstrated by Ritchie's *Eadarloch* dig
(1942). The outward shape of that site is hardly sharp-cornered, yet
there seems no doubt of the basic rectilinearity of the internal structure.

Ritchie was impressed by the apparent regularity of spacing of the
timbers, and made much of this in his interpretation. The present wri-
11 ter has reservations, however, since the site was not totally excavated.
3.14 The reconstruction drawings offered here should therefore not be re-
3.15 garded as definitive. They were made with computer aid to provide a
three-dimensional summary of the excavator's conclusions, as a basis

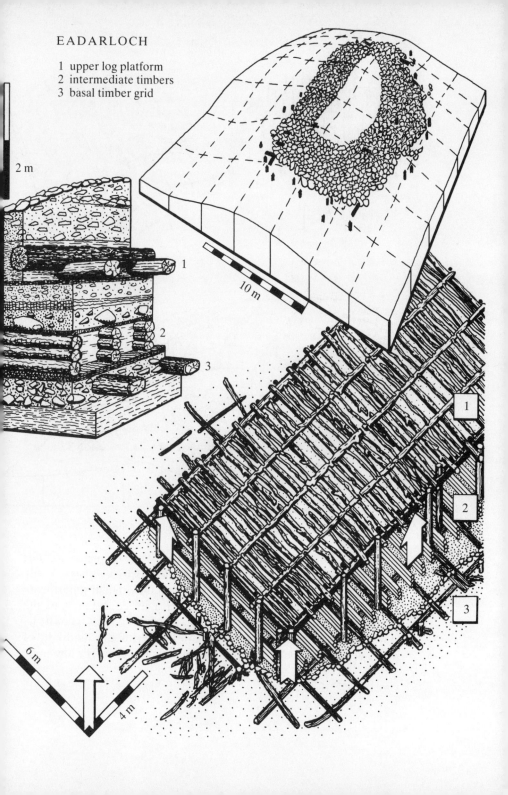

EADARLOCH

1 upper log platform
2 intermediate timbers
3 basal timber grid

2 m

10 m

1

2

3

6 m

4 m

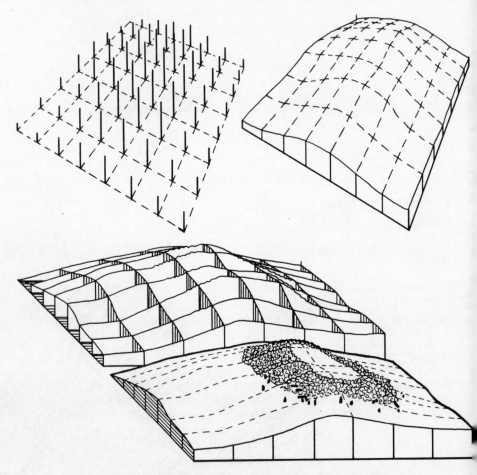

Figure 3.15. *Eadarloch.* Computer-aided construction of alternative views.

for discussion of a site that deserves re-excavation. It appears to offer a valuable contrast to the Milton Loch and Oakbank findings.

3.16   The striking isometric drawing included in the original report from Milton Loch (C.M.Piggott 1952–53) certainly contributed to the influence of that dig on subsequent crannog imagery. This reconstruction therefore merits careful consideration. With the hindsight of twenty years, it can be seen to present several problems. The low angle

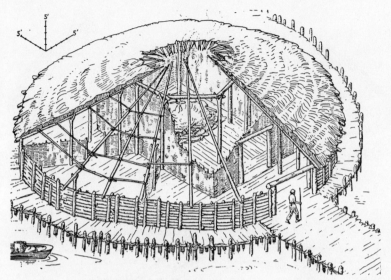

Figure 3.16. *Milton Loch I.* C. M. Piggott's isometric reconstruction.

of the roof does not accord with recent thinking on waterproof thatch (e.g. Drury ed. 1982), though a high-cocked roof would present problems on a gusty loch. More importantly, the drawing was prepared before it was realised that the site spanned at least seven centuries. From the state of Victorian jetties, it seems that the parts of piles exposed to wetting and drying do not last for much more than a century in Scottish lochs. Whether it was in continuous use or not, that site must therefore have been refurbished several times. With only two radiocarbon determinations and no dendrochronological work, we cannot know whether the elements of the site portrayed in the much-copied reconstruction ever existed simultaneously, or if not, in what order they figured. It would help to illuminate the history of the region as well as of the site itself to know about the relationship of the gang-way and canoe dock. Were they both in use simultaneously, in a peaceful exploitation of the resources of shore and lake? Or did one supersede the other, as the balance between security and convenience of access changed? If so, in what order did the changes occur, and how did their timing fit in with, say, the postulated Roman influence in the area? Wider considerations apart, the application of dendrochrono-

3.17

49

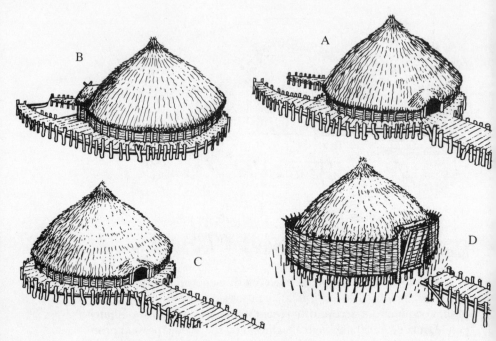

Figure 3.17. Alternative compromises between convenience and security.

logical techniques could have established whether the suggested internal partitions are feasible, and whether the outlying piles could legitimately be interpreted as one or more generations of supports for a continuous external walkway around the hut. As at *Eadarloch,* there is a case for re-excavation.

Considerations of these kinds have to be kept in mind at other sites too. This is certainly so regarding the possibility of finding that outlying piles extend the potential working area of a site, if this may change the range of functions for which it might conceivably be used. Piles rotted off flush with the lake bed are generally invisible from the surface and can be difficult for divers to find in mud, so it is reassuring that, at sites where numerous piles have in fact been detected, there is no suggestion of platforms as extensive as were once imagined over the Swiss lakes. *Faute de mieux,* mound size would appear to remain a reasonable criterion for basic comparisons of sites.

Figure 3.18. *Eadarloch:* A) after Ritchie; B) reinterpretation of piles as peripheral platform.

PROTECTION AND BUILDINGS. Not all outlying piles were necessarily used to support staging. Ritchie considered the possibility that those at *Eadarloch* were merely intended to break up incoming waves. 3.18 That seems unconvincing in view of their spacing and the position of the ladder there, and they may indeed have supported a peripheral platform (though as at Milton Loch, proof of synchronicity is required). Sometimes arrays of sharpened piles provided protection from human rather than wave attack. When the English assaulted a crannog near Omagh in AD 1566, going out on a raft, they found it

> so bearded with stakes and other sharp wood, as it was not without extreme difficulty scaleable, and so ramparted as if the hedge had been burned – for doing whereof the fireworks failed – without a long time it was not to be digged down. Yet some scaled to the top, whereof Edward Vaughan was one, who, being pushed with a pike from the same, fell . . . and being heavily armed – albeit he could swim perfectly well – was drowned. (Caulfield 1870)

It pays to keep your powder dry when confronting crannogers, and this type of *chevaux de frise* would clearly have been even more effective in the pre-gunpowder part of the crannog era. We should perhaps not altogether dismiss the possibility that the pile array at Milton Loch might represent a defensive hedge of 'sharp wood', rather than staging.

A late but outstanding pictorial source showing crannogs involved in strife exists in the Elizabethan war maps of Mountjoy's Irish campaign. The excellent work of the surveyor Richard Bartlett was more to our 3.19 advantage than his own. About the start of 1603, when he came into

51

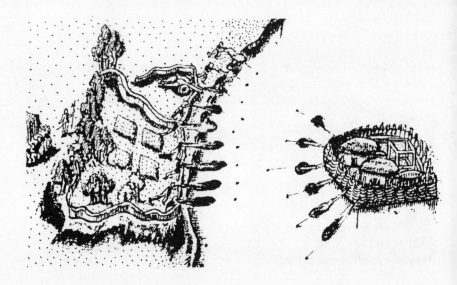

Figure 3.19. Irish crannogs, *c.*1600, re-drawn after Bartlett.

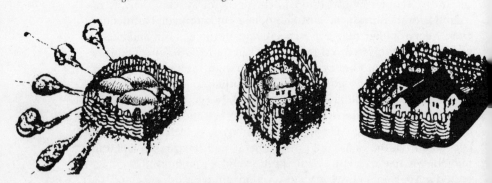

Tyrconnell 'the inhabitants took off his head, because they would not have their country discovered' (Cal. S. P. Ireland 1608–10, 280; Hayes-McCoy 1964). Bartlett shows several crannogs surrounded with stockades of what appears to be hurdling. One of the meanings Dwelly lists for *crannag* involves wickerwork frames. Could some such analogy underlie the adoption of the term for just such fastnesses in lakes and bogs? It would then refer to a visible characteristic rather than to the variable interior constitution of the mounds, and indeed would be compatible with Lacy's view that the island bases of some sites called crannogs in Donegal may not be artificial. Discussing the problem of etymology, Munro (1882) speculated whether *crann-* might apply to their wooden huts, rather than substructure, but it seems unlikely that, with wooden buildings common on shore, this would be taken up as the distinguishing characteristic of islet sites.

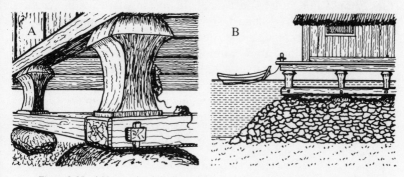

Figure 3.20. A) Norwegian joist-based structure; B) suggested crannog application.

Nowadays, little is to be seen of building remains on top of the islets, even where documentary or archaeological evidence of inhabitation is clear. Stony mounds often show neither stone wall footings nor evidence of major wooden uprights coming up through the boulder surface. Traditional wooden buildings evolved to cope with harsh environments can still be seen in Norway. These are often based on a horizontal frame of timbers set at, or indeed well above, ground level. 3.20 Such a system would have several advantages on crannogs. It could cope both with rocky islets resistant to pile driving, and with soft mounds where it was desirable to spread the load. As examples at Lom and Bigdøy show, it can facilitate good air circulation under the superstructure, inhibiting rot, and it is easy to add details that prevent vermin climbing up to get at crop-stores. In discussing old Scottish Gaelic terminology for *currachs,* Dwelly records the word *crannaghal* as meaning 'the framework'. In Scots, as in English, the definition of a joist is essentially that it is an horizontal structural timber, so the already-quoted account of Cumming's construction in Loch Lochy would appear to suggest that something akin to the Norwegian approach was among those used by Scots: 'This Lord builded ane Illand

53

. . . with four bigg oak Jests that were below in the water And he builded ane house thereupone . . .'.

Although visible remains of buildings are uncommon on the tops of the mounds, enough survives of the layout of some rectangular ones to suggest that insights into their functions may be obtained from the folk-life material of the recent past (e.g. Mitchell 1880, Grant 1961). One should not automatically equate rectangularity with recency, however. The Loch Glashan dig apparently showed a round hut superimposed on a rectangular one, and circular sheiling huts were to be seen in Scotland long after crannogs had dropped from view. Nevertheless, it seems reasonable to accept that, at the earlier end of their time range, round buildings were characteristic of the islets, as they were of most contemporary settlements on land. It is thus interesting to compare the size and layout of their round houses with representative sites from the Iron Age ashore.

ACCESS AND BOATS. At all periods, means of access are crucial to the functioning of an island site. When security was a prime consideration, and the moat effect was enhanced by fortifications, we may presume some form of controlled entrance. Rynne and MacEoin (1978) have found both archaeological and literary support for the Craggaunowen replica gatehouse. Lord Cumming's Lochaber *oubliette* would hardly have worked without a narrow and probably dark entry to the house. Gangways to the shore being at once a convenience and a risk, drawbridges are not inconceivable. Where stone causeways are reported, early writers sometimes speculated that they lay originally beneath the surface, and that gaps and zig-zags might have been traps for unwary waders . . . . This may well be correct, but some of the strips of submerged rubble that are described as causeways do not look as if they ever offered good footing, however knowledgeable the wader. Lobes sticking out from crannog mounds, though they may have the plan configuration of jetties or little docks, are also often lower than seems functional, and also consist of tumbled stones rather than suggesting a useful working surface. Sometimes wooden piles may be detected around their periphery. Mediterranean fishermen still build up narrow jetties by containing rocks within crude woodwork. In attempting interpretations, we should perhaps keep in mind that what we are seeing may be the residue of collapsed composite

Plate 10. Dr Nick Dixon excavating *Oakbank* crannog.

Plate 11. *Eadarloch.* Upper Log Platform excavated by Ritchie.

Plate 12. *Milton Loch I.* Foundation timbers under excavation by C. M. Piggott.

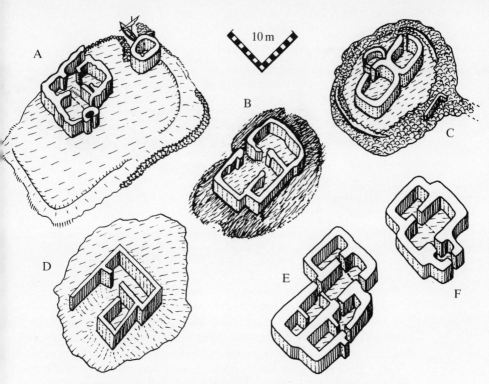

Figure 3.21. Comparison of rectangular buildings on built-up islets with traditional black house and other Highland house type: A) Loch a'Phearsain, Argyll; B) Loch of Leys, near Banchory; c) Loch nan Cinneachan, Coll; D) Loch Arthur/Lotus, Kirkcudbright; E) Black house at Callanish; F) Mitchell's older house-type.

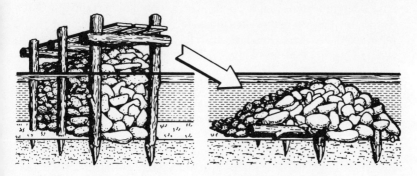

Figure 3.22. Timber and rubble breakwater, before/after collapse.

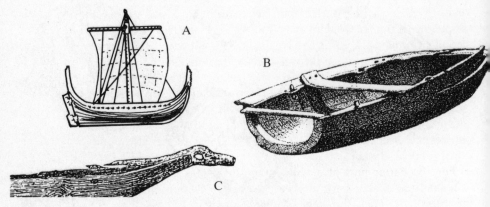

Figure 3.23. A) Hieland gallay, MacLeod tomb, *Rodel,* Harris 1528; B) The *Dowalton* boat (6.4 m); c) *Loch Lotus* canoe (13.7 m), made *ca* ad 30 ± 80 (allowing for position in log of s r r-403, 100 bc ± 80).

constructions, rather than stone features *per se.*

Though docks are not common, log boats of various kinds have been found in direct association with several crannogs, and even incorporated in their structure. One made from an oak log but with added washboard strake, transom, thole-pins and thwart, was found under the edge of one of the Dowalton crannogs in Wigtonshire, 'in the foundations of the island, with hurdles and planks above it' (Stuart 1866, 5). Had superstructure collapsed upon it, or was a redundant boat merely being recycled as fill, as elsewhere? It was 21 feet (6.4 m) long, but others hollowed from single logs up to 45 feet (13.7 m) long have been reported from the beds of lochs containing crannogs. Often we do not know whether specific canoes belonged to crannog users, but since the earliest known Scottish log boat, from Friarton by Perth, is dated stratigraphically to before 8000 bp, and the latest was apparently in use in Moidart in the eighteenth century A D (MacDonald 1889), there seems little doubt about their availability to early and late crannog users, wherever there was suitable timber.

Lightweight skin-covered craft are much more elusive archaeologically, but their use in Scotland can again be shown to more than span the crannog era, running from at least the early Bronze Age (Watkins 1980) to the eighteenth century A D (Fenton 1972). There is an account (Clanranald 1819) of their use in a fifteenth-century raid on Loch Moy to seize the Mackintosh from his island castle, which had a satellite crannog as a prison. (Those were troubled waters: the cunning Cummings are said to have dammed up the loch to flood them out.) We will be lucky to recover the fragile remains of currachs or coracles from crannog excavations. The spreads of fine stones flooring the 'docks' and on the flanks of some of the sites surveyed in Loch Awe are, however, intriguing. Jagged rocks could damage a skin-covered craft. One wonders if the gravel was laid to facilitate beaching *crannaghal*? (Besides meaning its framework, the word can also signify 'the frail boat' itself.)

For the better part of a millennium during the crannog period, sophisticated clinker-built boats were a major element in the power politics of the Highlands and Islands (Steer and Bannerman 1977, Morrison 1981a, c). To a society equipped with the various species of *'lumphaddis, birlingis* and *Hieland gallayis'* the long lochs of the Highlands offered better highways than much of the intervening terrain. This must have conditioned the outlook of islet users to the landscape around them.

In *The Idea of History,* Collingwood criticised those who wrote in too facile a way of 'the influence of geography on history', suggesting that

> the fact that certain people live on an island has in itself no effect on their history; what has an effect is the way they conceive that insular position; whether for example they regard the sea as a barrier or as a highway . . . it will produce one effect if they have not mastered the art of navigation, a different effect if they have mastered it better than their neighbours, a third if they have mastered it worse . . . (1946, 200)

As we have seen, even in the 'historical' period, we have little more direct access to the minds of the islet-users than in the fully prehistoric era. It is with caveats such as these very much before us that we turn to consider what may be learnt from the relationship of the sites to their settings in the lochs and landscape.

4. Loch and Landscape

Writing of Scotland, Stuart Piggott has suggested on more than one occasion (Piggott 1958, 1; Piggott and Ritchie 1982) that
> to understand a people, one must first understand their country. Without a knowledge of the routes of access and of egress by land and sea, of the regions of mountain and moorland over against those of forest and flood plain, of the conditions of climate and natural environment – in a word, without a geographical setting – any study of human communities in past or present times must be a meaningless abstraction.

Earlier investigators of crannogs tended to look at them as individual entities. There was little systematic exploration of possible relationships with environmental factors or with other islets and sites ashore. This was the case in almost all studies prior to 1970. Nowadays, we try to view archaeological sites in the perspective of their landscape setting, seeking to understand them as components in whole systems of interacting cultural, economic and environmental elements. In attempting this wider view, today's investigators share with those of the past the problem of shortage of dating evidence. It does seem reasonable to accept that several islet and land sites would tend to be in use simultaneously in any given loch basin, and sometimes this can be demonstrated directly (chapter 2, and below). But while specific dating evidence remains so sparse, it seems injudicious to use distribution maps to speculate on such topics as prehistoric 'chieftainship areas'. It is clearly premature to claim definitive relationships before strict contemporaneity can be proved. The intention in this essay is more limited; it is to draw attention to juxtapositions and patterns in the landscape that prompt questions for further investigation. The present research strategy was designed as an inexpensive approach to two complementary aims: to develop a policy for the systematic acquisition of dates; and to lay a foundation for more sophisticated analyses of distributions.

As geographers have learnt over the last decade or so, powerful tools of spatial analysis will not yield much if applied in a naïve way to difficult historical and environmental evidence (Norton 1984, Gatrell 1983, Hodder and Orton 1976). It is over-optimistic to embark on ambitious quantitative analyses of distributions, until the basic characteristics of the data have been thoroughly explored. This is not only a matter of appreciating factors conditioning the survival of what is mapped. The choice of analytical models can be crucial. Many incorporate assumptions about boundaries or terrain that make them too abstract for present purposes: Scotland is not a boundless isotropic plane. Furthermore, as Butzer (1982) has discussed in general terms, and Fojut (1982) in a specifically Scottish case, there are technical problems in dealing statistically with archaeological distributions in relation to natural systems with particular kinds of boundaries, such as the water bodies, drainage basins and islands that concern us here. Cultural aspects are also involved in any analyses of crannog distributions, or in individual site-catchment studies. Account has to be taken of the probability that the lifestyles of most (but not, as Collingwood emphasised, necessarily all) islet users predisposed them towards water transport. Finger lochs offer competent boatmen tens of kilometres of fast routes through some of the most difficult terrain in Scotland, though only on particular axes. While the use made of such routes may have varied through time, the geographical pattern of such opportunities is relatively stable. Other elements in the landscape are more susceptible to change, even from decade to decade, and at present we often lack the dating evidence needed to relate their detailed variations to the occupation period of specific crannogs.

It therefore seems best to start by looking at the relationship of sites to the relatively unchanging elements in the landscape's potential for human use. When Piggott proposed that physical aspects of the terrain were fundamental, this was in the sense that these offered a sensible starting point. In *Scotland before History* he went on to develop an holistic view of the interactions between peoples and their environments, not a deterministic one. Similarly, our aim here is to begin by identifying the basic physical constraints on islet builders and users, so that having established these as a lowest common denominator in placing crannogs, we can secure a clearer view of the less tangible but no less important human criteria in locational decisions; what Childe

59

once called the 'ideas [that] form as effective an element in the environment of any human society as . . . external nature' (1942, 14).

The Immediate Setting

The built-up islets of Scotland are to be found in a great variety of water bodies, from arms of the sea, as at Eriska or Beauly, to rivers and estuaries. The great majority are in inland waters, which themselves vary from mere marshes and ponds to major lochs. Some of these experience greater storm waves than the sheltered marine sites.

The geomorphological factors in lake genesis show a broad regional patterning. Thus, although divisions are not absolute, the most characteristic types of lochs do vary across Scotland. This has implications for the nature of the archaeological sites likely to be associated with them. The Western and Northern Isles are characterised by glacially scoured rock basins, with rock knob islets. As we have seen, these offer solid foundations suitable for heavy superstructures, in an area where there has always been a tendency to build in stone because of the shortage of timber throughout the Holocene (Birks 1977). Some basins there have however filled up with soft mud or peat. In the Lowlands, as in the Isles, most lakes are shallow. Some are in erosional basins, but many lie in uneven glacial and fluvioglacial deposits, such as drumlin hollows and kettleholes. Clay, gravel or mud bottoms are common, though rock is exposed too. There are plenty of small lochs on the mainland north of the Highland line, too, but most characteristic there are big trough lakes, where major bedrock structures have been picked out by the many episodes of Pleistocene glaciation.

Throughout Scotland, the lake environment is by no means a fossil one, surviving unchanged from the Ice Age until recent modification by man. It is a dynamic system, with biological cycles and sedimentation regimes proceeding differently from lake to lake, and even varying within the same lake. Factors such as wind-driven currents keep some areas clear of sediment, while others have considerable mud accumulation (Morrison 1973a,b, 1980a). The characteristics of lacustrine environments thus cannot be taken for granted. Their study is a necessary background to the appraisal of the archaeology of crannogs. Happily the pioneer bathymetric survey by Sir John Murray (chapter 5) created a foundation that has encouraged research ever since his day, so the Scottish lakes are remarkably well represented in

the international scientific literature. Let us now consider basic constraints on island building.

WATER DEPTH. It is difficult to be precise about the maximum depth
of water considered feasible by the builders. Building was certainly
limited to the shallows, but because of possible changes in the lochs,
we can seldom be sure about the water level at the time when an individual crannog was being built. Some indication of what depth was
acceptable may be gained from the vertical amplitude of the structures, although it is difficult to establish what allowance should be
made for wooden superstructures lost from the top, as well as for
compaction and subsidence. In the Loch Awe survey, the remains of
at least a quarter of the sites were more than 4.5 m tall. One stood over
8 m high, though it was banked up against a bedrock reef. In general
5 m is a much more usual limit in Scotland. It seems safe to assume that
crannogs are unlikely where the original bottom depth was more than
10 m. Indeed, half of those observed in Loch Awe were under 2 m tall.
These included several of those farthest offshore, lying between 100
and 200 m out. This brings out the crannogers' penchant for saving
work by finding and capping pre-existing shoals.

FOUNDATIONS. Although natural hummocks seem to have been posi-
tively sought out, extensive steep slopes were impracticable. These
are not uncommon, particularly in Highland lochs. In places, glacial
erosion carved the sides of the troughs into near vertical cliffs. Offshore profiles can plunge to depths of a hundred metres or more, only
tens of metres out from the bank. Even in less extreme cases, glaciers
sometimes left rock slopes near to the maximum angle of rest for
saturated sediments. Mud that settles there tends to build up until it
slumps away into the depths, sometimes in the form of a turbidity
current (Morrison 1973a,b). Even had there been good reasons for
wanting a crannog in such a location, the gradient would have been too
steep for it to hold under its own weight, and the bedrock would not
accept piles to anchor it. There is scope for investigating how builders
solved the contrasting engineering problems of coping both with sites
on beds too hard for pile driving, and with others in very soft deposits.
The general preference seems to have been for areas of stability with
a firm substrate (gravel, till or rock) that would not be subject to com-

61

paction under the weight of the crannog. In some cases, however, it is apparent that other factors in the choice of a site have made builders willing to accept foundation problems. Thus some of the crannogs both in the Highlands and Lowlands consist of a thin raft of logs and stones on top of a considerable thickness of soft Holocene muds; and like Milton Loch Crannog I, they quake if leapt upon. These contrast with the sheer solidity characteristic of many other crannog sites, which incorporate hundreds of tons of boulders and very substantial timbers. As noted in chapter 3, sometimes sites within sight of each other have been built on quite different principles, one perhaps in sediment with considerable use of piling, and another on a bedrock ridge where pile-driving was impossible.

SHELTER. The hazards presented by wave attack were certainly a factor in selecting locations for crannogs. The sheer size of many of Scotland's lochs has to be realised to appreciate the severity of conditions that can develop upon them in summer squalls, let alone a week of November gales. The shape of the glens tends to exacerbate matters. The interplay of linear geological structures with glacial erosion produced their characteristically trough-like form, and their orientation (commonly conforming to 'the Caledonian trend') often coincides with the prevailing south-westerly winds. Even where this is not so, the size of the valleys is often sufficient to channel local surface winds along the length of the loch. About 380 of Scotland's lochs are more than a kilometre long; some 65 more than 5 km, and 19 more than 10 km. Loch Tay is over 23 km long, with an area of 26 sq. km, and both Ness and Lomond are over 35 km long with areas of 56 and 71 sq. km respectively. The effect on leeward shores of gales blowing along the length of such lochs is impressive, and dangerous.

4.1   Loch Awe has an area of 38 sq. km, and is over 40 km long. The dominant wind and wave direction is along the length of the trough from the south-west, and it is notable that three-quarters of its twenty crannogs have been placed in locations that afford shelter from that direction. Of those few sites that are less well protected, two lie off long stretches of shoreline that do not offer the option of more sheltered sites. Only one seemingly unnecessarily flouts the principle of protection from south-westerlies. It lies on the exposed side of the peninsula of *Ceann Mara*. With better-sheltered sites unused nearby,

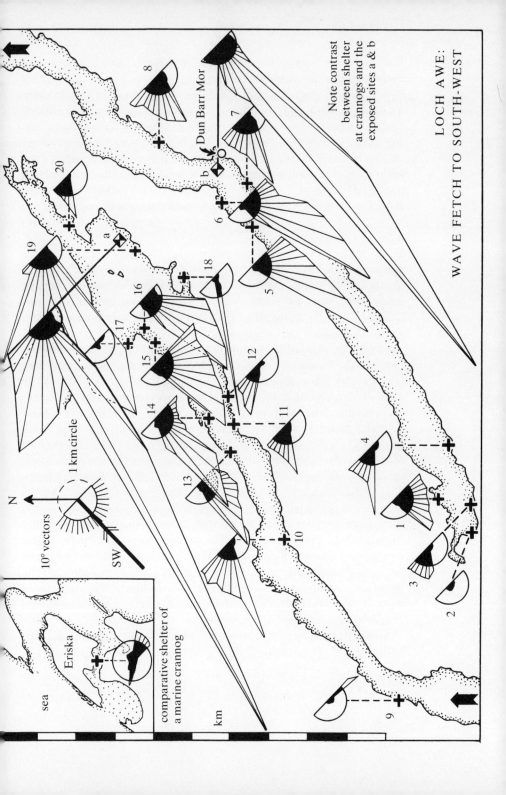

LOCH AWE:

WAVE FETCH TO SOUTH-WEST

Note contrast
between shelter
at crannogs and the
exposed sites a & b

Dun Barr Mor

10° vectors

1 km circle

N

SW

comparative shelter of
a marine crannog

Eriska

sea

km

it would be interesting to know what human priorities were reflected in this apparently anomalous placing.

Not only the location, but the detailed layout of sites often takes account of wind and weather. In Loch Awe, the best developed harbour is on an islet lying over 200 m offshore. It is on the side sheltered from south-west gales, as are the little boat docks and jetties on the other sites. At Ederline (Morrison 1981b) an extension of the bedrock reef around which the crannog is built seems to have been used as a breakwater. Rocks have been piled on it and several major blocks, apparently washed off the top, lie immediately to leeward.

Patterns in the Landscape

Waterbodies do not have unique points that are the only feasible places for building a crannog, so whilst the physical conditions within the lochs clearly conditioned the decisions of the islet builders, in most cases there must have remained considerable latitude in the final choice of site. By examining how that latitude was used we may gain some insights into their intentions.

4.2   Some crannogs are placed as far from shore as physically practic-
4.5c,d able, on the outermost edges of shelves. Others are tucked into snug corners only a few metres offshore, where a fire-arrow could easily have reached the thatch. This suggests a spectrum of attitudes, with differing priorities for security and convenience. At fishing and fowling stations, security might be irrelevant. Other islets may have been primarily a method of protecting produce or livestock from four-footed vermin, great and small, rather than from human enemies. A crannog could be effectively rodent-proofed; and even bears (probably present to AD 1000) might be more easily repelled. Wolves persisted in Scotland until the eighteenth century, so stockmen would have slept sounder with their beasts in an offshore byre, like that found at Oakbank. As suggested above, in many cases we may suspect compromises between convenience for mundane functions in normal times, and some provision for security in occasional emergencies. The historical records leave no doubt that their role was often identified with human strife. It will be recalled that the legislation of 1608 bracketed 'houssis of defence strongholdis and cranokis'.

Security might be of a passive kind (as many envisage was the case with brochs), or it might be for those with aggression in mind, as at

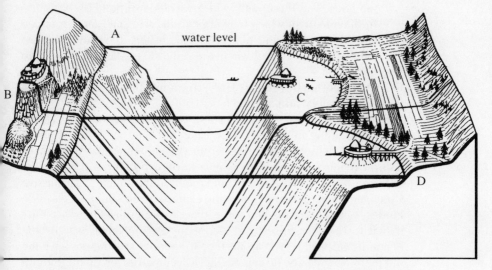

Figure 4.2. Summary of landscape criteria in siting on a deep loch. A) Shallow ledge under water, but no arable potential: generally no site; B) good land, but too steep offshore: dun a possibility; C, D) shallow shelf, good land: offshore (C) or inshore (D) sites, choice depending on hazard perception.

Loch Lochy where we have seen that not only the Cummings but their rivals the Mackintoshes built and garrisoned islets as strongpoints, seeking to dominate the region. There are hints that in both passive and aggressive cases, some island-builders chose a site to exploit the inaccessibility of the area where a loch lay, as well as the water barrier itself. Sanctuary of this kind seems to be the aim of the built-up islet in *Loch nam Ban Mòra*, the Loch of the Big Women, high up the Sgurr of Eigg. Other islets built in remote Highland fastnesses were traditionally robber's roosts (e.g. Loch nan Torran and Loch Tullah in Argyll, Loch Lundie in Inverness-shire).

While some are characterised by isolation as well as literal insulation, many other built-up islets in fact lie near quite substantial settlements on shore or on larger islands. Historical statements bearing specifically on relationships between them are few, late and difficult to substantiate. Typical is that by Grose (1797), regarding the isle of Friar's Carse near Dumfries:

Here was a cell dependent on the rich abbey of Melrose . . . near the house was the Lough, which was the fish-pond of the friary. In the middle of which is a very curious artificial island, founded upon large piles and planks of oak, where the monks lodged their valuable effects when the English made an inroad into Strathnith.

Diggings reported by Munro (1890) confirmed the construction of the island, but proved little more.

Even traditions are scarce. This is where one particularly regrets the dearth of dating information. Consider the site off Ardchonnell in Loch Awe. It is located as far from the shoreline and the nearby natural island as possible. It is in a fairly exposed position, on the outermost edge of the shallows, and required the building of a massive stone and timber mound (this is the example over 8 m tall). Was it to hinder ingress or egress that it was placed so far out? One possibility is that it was a precursor, not a contemporary, of the castle on the bigger island, and served as a refuge for people who did not have the numbers or capacity to defend the larger perimeter of the natural island. Innis Chonnell castle goes back at least to the thirteenth century (RCAHMS Argyll vol.2, 233). Another possibility is that it was built later, as an adjunct to the castle, and the aim may have been to make it difficult to get off rather than onto the islet, i.e. it may have been equivalent to the artificial Prison Island built adjacent to the Castle Island of Loch Kinord, Aberdeenshire.

Although the available historical records are tantalisingly incomplete, they alert us to the diverse purposes for which small islands might serve as satellites to larger establishments: ranging from isolating fire-risks on a Kitchen Island, to keeping hounds out of mischief (Loch Laggan and the Lake of Menteith each have an *Eilean nan Con* or Dog Island). Kennel-islands were close by home bases, but the hunt itself might well take place much further off. Hunting-lodges remind us that, just as juxtaposition is no proof of relationship, neither is isolation evidence of independence of function. Many studies of the prehistoric and the recent past (e.g. Selinge 1979, Borchgrevinck 1980, Morrison 1983) have drawn attention to the wide range of roles for specialised out-stations located at a distance from the home base, many used by only part of the community, and for only part of the year.

The island hunting-lodges and feasting-houses of Scotland and Ireland offer an attractive field for research (Gilbert 1979). They figure in early records of the great Highland families (e.g. Gordon 1630), and some of the islets so used are certainly artificial (as in Lochs Brora and Kinellan, and Eadarloch). These were something different from simple fishing and fowling stations. Food bones from such Country Club Crannogs underline their recreational role, being dominantly of domestic beasts rather than those of the chase. The roisterers in a *Tigh nam Fleadh* (House of Feasts) were not so injudicious as to rely on their prowess with the bow.

That was the Gaelic name used of the *Eadarloch* site, but it was not the only one associated with it. The kind of insights lost with the general demise of Gaelic is emphasised by what may be gleaned there. *Eadarloch* is unusual because it is represented both in oral material written down in earlier centuries, and in traditions that Ritchie (1942) collected in the 1930s, helped by Professor W.J.Watson. The site features in *A'Chomhachag,* or The Houlet's Sang, a patchwork of Gaelic verse surviving from the threshold of the seventeenth century, and referring to the pleasures of the hunt in that neighbourhood (Mackechnie 1946, Rankine 1958). It seems that the crannog was repaired by Raonull Gòrach, chief of Keppoch from 1554 to 1587, and it has been suggested that much of the poem reflects the failure of the poet Donald Mackinlay to be admitted to one of that chief's feasts on the island, leading him to commune with the ancient Owl of Strone on his way home . . .

Ma dh' fhàgadh Dòmhnall a muigh
'Na aonar aig tigh nam fleadh
Is gèarr a bhios gucag air bhuil . . .
[If Donald has been left alone outside at the house of feasts,
   there won't be froth (on the drink) for long . . .]

Be that as it may, an 1878 Gaelic account notes 'this island is the site of Tigh nam Fleadh, and there MacMhicRaghnaill used to hold any special meeting with the nobles of the district' (Diarmad 1876, 330). The latter was a Keppoch, and Blundell (1909–10) heard it referred to as 'Keppoch's Council Island'. In the 1930s it was still known as *Eilean na Comhairle* (Council Island), or as the Treaty Island, with a story that when two chiefs had a dispute, they came up on opposite sides of the loch and swam to the island to settle their differences. This tale may well be recent romancing around the traditional name, but there are other suggestions of Highland customs analogous to the

67

formalised *holm ganga* of the Sagas (Morrison 1978c). To a clan society that set such store by territoriality, an artificial islet might be valued as a neutral site for negotiators to meet, in that it need not be considered a natural part of any clan's land. It would be interesting to find if any Irish evidence bears on this.

The Eadarloch site was also known traditionally as *Eilean Ruighe na Slighe,* the Island of the Sheiling of the Track, and Ritchie draws attention to the provision of 'spittals' (hospices) as secure stop-over points for travellers in the Highlands. The site is adjacent to *An'Dèbhadh,* a natural sand-spit offering a crossing place between Loch Treig and Eadarloch, on the old route between Glen Spean and Rannoch. That some islets were installed at points where land routes took to the water gains support elsewhere. It is perhaps not surprising that provision should be made to serve, guard or control crossings. Nor is it only fords and boat ferries that have to be taken into account. Haldane (1973) makes it clear that even in the recent past it was common practice to swim herds across lochs and even sea straits, such as that between Skye and the mainland. He notes that latter-day drovers were merely following their less reputable ancestors, quoting Mackintosh of Borlum's description of reivers at Kenmore, each man gripping a bullock's tail as

> he drove into the water and extends out his other hand with his fusee and his pistol in his teeth, and so is drawn with his firearms dry to the other side . . . (p.39)

The 40-km length of Loch Awe lay athwart just such traditional cattle routes. Three built-up islets appear anomalous, in that they lack the local arable base which is characteristic there. However, they seem well placed if considered as possible swimming stations for beasts. Two are at constrictions in the loch where side valleys offer routes across the general north-east/south-west 'grain' of the country. A third lies off Kilneuaire, which became a major nodal point in the cattle-droving pattern.

4.3   Munro and some of the other early workers were puzzled by the role of sites in the Dumbuck area of the Clyde estuary, and wondered if they played some part in navigation or river crossing. In evaluating these sites, we must remember the extent to which the navigable chan-

Figure 4.3. Clyde estuary sites, with Munro's 'queer things of the Clyde', plus genuine brooch and comb. (Site location off Antonine Wall, courtesy Helen Adamson.)

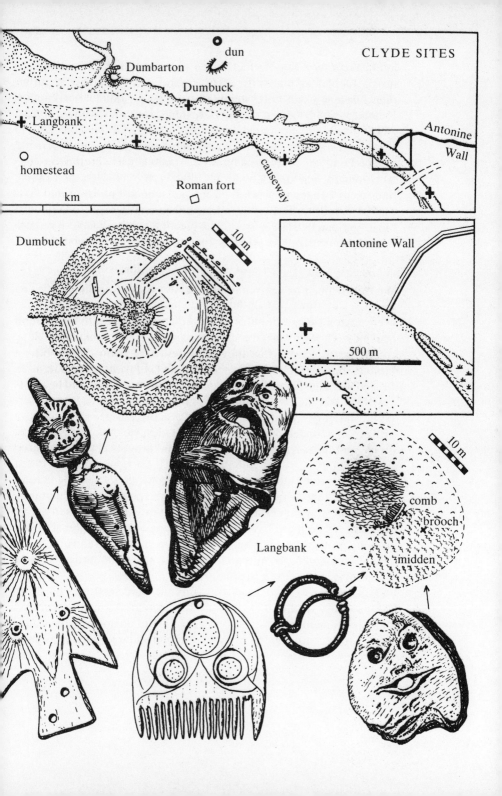

CLYDE SITES

dun

Dumbarton

Dumbuck

Langbank

homestead

km

Roman fort

causeway

Antonine Wall

Dumbuck

10 m

Antonine Wall

500 m

10 m

comb

brooch

midden

Langbank

nel of the Clyde is a product of the eighteenth and nineteenth centuries. As Riddell put it, the early importance of Dumbarton, rather
than Glasgow, as a port 'stemmed from its proximity to a shoal at
Dumbuck which formed the effective limit of navigation on the Clyde'
(1979, 8). Until the late eighteenth century (Macdonald 1932) the
Clyde was fordable there on foot. The dating of the Dumbuck and
13   nearby Langbank sites was obscured by salting with spurious antiquities (roundly denounced by Munro, 1905). But amongst the genuine
finds from Langbank was a La Tène penannular brooch of mid first-
century date (Stevenson 1966). It would be very interesting to know if
the as-yet-undated site opposite the end of the Antonine Wall is there
by mere coincidence, or whether there was a functional relationship.

Agriculture and the Loch Sites

We clearly need to keep in mind a wide range of possibilities when
seeking to interpret the possible uses of built-up islands. There is, however, a strong suggestion that many were associated with agricultural
activities. Though some crannogs are located in such high and bleak
country as to suggest that they were never the permanent abode of
farmers, most seem to be located close to land with arable potential.
In the Highlands as well as in the Lowlands, excavations and field surveys bear out the commonness of agricultural connections. It is certainly proper to regard some crannogs as actual farmsteads. Digs have
provided a rounded picture of their activities, yielding the remains of
crops, and indeed of wooden ploughs and ards. Oakbank produced
4.4   one possibility; another came from Milton Loch, and it may be that
the object recovered from the Loch Kielziebar site by Mapleton's
divers (1870) was another. Bones and byre deposits from domestic
animals have also been reported from sites widely dispersed across
Scotland, while there have been indications of many of the activities
that one would expect in a homestead, from the storage and processing
of crops (and gathered nuts and fruits), through spinning and weaving
to smithing.

The Loch Awe and Loch Tay surveys were mounted partly to
explore the agricultural element in site location. As indicated above,
these investigations took in the whole basins of the lochs to the watershed, with attention being paid to their land and water connections to
neighbouring basins. At the present stage of reconnaisance, more

Plate 13. *Dumbuck* crannog. The original excavators, who turned up Munro's 'queer things of the Clyde'.

Plate 14. Problems of excavation: boulders overlying vulnerable timbers, *Oakbank*.

Plate 15. Quality of survival: tool marks on pile-point from *Oakbank* (scale in cm).

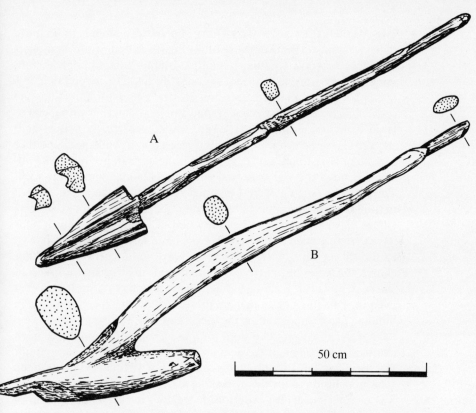

Figure 4.4. A) *Milton Loch I*: ard (400 bc ± 100, κ-1394); B) *Oakbank*: possible plough (after G. Thomas, courtesy N. Dixon).

seems likely to be learned by a comparative approach within and between basins, than by treating sample sites in isolation. It was also felt that site catchment analyses based on a radius of a given *walking* time would have serious limitations when dealing with lifestyles so intimately involved with access by water. It seemed arbitrary and premature to allot theoretical equivalents for relative ease of land and water movement until more was known about boat types and how they were used. Awe and Tay were selected to help redress the bias in previous studies towards small lochs in the south-west of Scotland. They contained a similar number of sites (about twenty each), but differed sufficiently to suggest that comparisons would be rewarding.

71

THE LAKE-VILLAGE HYPOTHESIS. Lochs very often contain more than one built-up islet. Because of the dearth of dating information, it is difficult to know whether a multiple-islet loch might imply a community of lake dwellers. In smaller ones, such as Dowalton Loch, it is unclear whether the proximity of sites reflects any more than the restricted size of the waterbody. One aim in attempting a total cull of large lochs, such as Awe and Tay, was to see whether sites there showed signs of clustering, given the greater area available. In neither loch were sites found set together with the appearance of a 'lake village'. Instead they lie scattered along the whole length of the loch.

4.5A   Towards the north-east end of Loch Awe there is an abundance of natural islets of morainic material that offers a ready-made basis for a village cluster, if that had been the aim. The larger of these islands have certainly been used. *Fraoch Eilan* has a castle going back at least to the thirteenth century (RCAHMS Argyll vol.2) as well as a later church. *Inishail's* burial ground contains an Early Christian cross-slab. There is, however, little sign of activity on the other natural islets. Yet even in their immediate neighbourhood labour has been invested in building five crannogs along the loch's east and west shores.

A mid-lake village, clustered for mutual support, would have been an obvious stratagem if the demands of defence had been paramount. But the overall distribution pattern in Loch Awe seems to point to the same conclusion as the detailed siting of the built islets: while security was obviously a major criterion in building in the water, it did not over-ride all other factors. When the sparse use of this readily available group of natural islets is set against the sheer amount of work involved in constructing the twenty Loch Awe crannogs, it seems clear that their builders must have had strong reasons for preferring sites elsewhere in the loch.

Although the locations they chose run from end to end of the waterbody, they are not evenly dispersed. In some cases three or four lie within a few hundred metres of each other, while others are separated by five or six kilometres. We do not yet know whether particular sites were contemporary. However, with twenty involved, it would be surprising if there were not overlaps in date. Thus some of the groupings and discontinuities in the pattern may reflect siting decisions based on considerations such as family alliances or antagonisms, inaccessible to us in the absence of documents or oral traditions. The irregular dis-

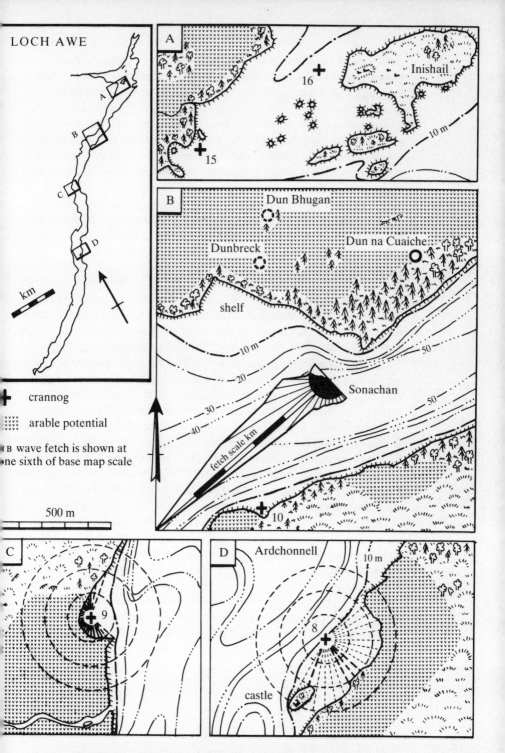

LOCH AWE

A

16

15

Inishail

10 m

B

Dun Bhugan

Dunbreck

Dun na Cuaiche

shelf

10 m

20

30

40

50

50

Sonachan

fetch scale km

10

C

9

D

Ardchonnell

10 m

8

castle

km

✚ crannog

⋮⋮⋮ arable potential

B wave fetch is shown at one sixth of base map scale

500 m

Figure 4.5. *Loch Awe* sites: relationships to lake and landscape.

tribution of the crannogs nevertheless follows a pattern that seems sufficiently marked to identify at least one criterion fundamental to their builders' selection of locations: availablility of arable land.

RELATION TO FARMABLE LAND. As elsewhere in Scotland many islets seem to have been sited in relation to patches of farmable land. One reason for choosing Loch Awe was that the marked variations of land-use potential along its shores would help to clarify any such relationship. Considerable areas within its valley have minimal soil cover over ice-scoured bedrock. The areas with till, fluvioglacial deposits or recent alluvium of reasonable agricultural potential are often localised and sharply defined. In most cases it is possible to be reasonably confident that the basic layout of these deposits has not changed significantly during the Holocene.

The disposition of the crannogs relative to both the positive and the negative aspects of land-quality around the loch supports the hypothesis that their builders were much concerned with immediate access to the better patches of land. Thus, stretches of shore backed by rough rocky country tend to be crannog-free (there are gaps of c. 8 km and 6 km, and many shorter instances), while the great majority of sites are indeed closely juxtaposed to patches of viable soil. Because of the current importance of commercial forestry, the present land use pattern of the area is unrepresentative of its potential for subsistence agriculture. The site pattern was therefore compared with land-use surveys made in the earlier part of this century. The majority of crannogs were adjacent to land that was either being actively worked up to the 1930s as arable, or was then classified as good quality meadowland. Field inspection suggested the latter had arable potential, and under the grass old rigs could sometimes be made out, confirming this. In all, seventeen of the twenty built-up islets in Loch Awe can be said to lie immediately adjacent to patches of land of arable potential.

Given this percentage, it might seem tempting to base a population model for the basin on the sizes of the sites, along with the areas of the farmable patches. This would be unwise. First, although the distribution may support the suggestion that the sites reflect agricultural activity on the adjacent land, they were not necessarily all homesteads. Excavation is needed to establish whether some were, say, secure stores rather than dwellings, or served other ancillary roles for the

74

farming community. Secondly, until more dates become available, the possibility remains that with the restricted size of the isolated patches of farmable land, a site might be used until the land there was worked out, when the crannogers might have moved off along the loch to assart another patch, and build a new islet.

With such a high degree of association between built-up islets and land quality, one may enquire why the remaining patches of good land around Loch Awe lack crannogs. In some cases, part of the answer lies underwater. At Braevallich and in stretches on both sides of the loch near Sonachan, the loch bed plunges away from the shoreline of the arable land in a steep and unstable underwater slope, leading straight into very deep water. In places such as these, islet building was impracticable. In part of the Sonachan area, the precipitous underwater   4.5B slopes are replaced by a wide shallow shelf; but this is open to southwesterly storms, with a long wave fetch down the length of the loch. No trace of crannogs was in fact found on that shelf. It is interesting that a cluster of *dun* names is located there, in the area of the arable land close to the shore (*Dun Bhugan, Dunbreck* and *Dun na Cuaiche*: RCAHMS Argyll vol.2, 88, no.180). This is an unusual placing in the Loch Awe basin, where few duns or dun names occur low down near the loch side. The dun at *Barr Mor* is another such exception. This is   4.1 on a hillock rising 20 m above the loch, by a pocket of arable land at the mouth of the Kames River. The offshore profile drops steeply into deep water there, and that bay is the terminus for waves with a fetch of ten kilometres from the south-west. As at Sonachan, this again seems no place to build a crannog, and none was in fact found.

A complementary aspect of the pattern at Loch Awe is that neither remains of duns nor dun names are characteristic of the patches of farmable land off which crannogs lie. As indicated in chapter 3, there are uncertainties in estimating the usable areas of crannogs from their mound sizes. Nevertheless, the broad limits for the Loch Awe set are apparent, and it is interesting that where duns are found there instead of crannogs, their internal dimensions are of the same general order   4.6 (e.g. *Dun na Cuaiche*, 12.2 × 11.4 m; dun at *Barr Mor*, 29 × 19 m).

Overall, then, it seems worth considering the hypothesis that, in some periods at least, those who required a secure base adjacent to their farmland might elect to build either a dun or a crannog, their choice being in part conditioned by relative advantages of sites and

75

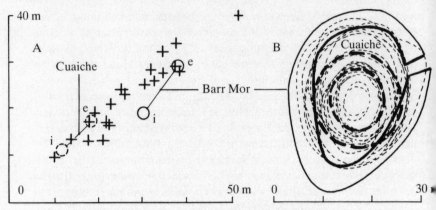

Figure 4.6. A) Sizes of Loch Awe crannogs and duns (i = interior, e = exterior of duns Barr Mor and na Cuaiche); B) Duns and crannog mound-top plans superimposed.

materials that were available locally, on land and in the water.

The Loch Tay area further illustrates both the desirability and the difficulty of studying crannogs as an integral part of regional patterns, rather than in isolation from other activities in the landscape. In a methodological paper, Stevenson (1975) considered relationships between different forms of modern land-use and the preservation and discovery of sites. He suggested that the Loch Tay basin seemed under-represented in field monuments, compared to the valley of the River Tay to the east. He did not, however, include the crannogs. Though mentioned in local sources (Gillies 1938), these had not then been confirmed by the Dixon survey. Adding them to his map redresses the overall balance. There remains, however, a marked contrast in the number of sites that may be homesteads, as represented on shore in the Loch Tay basin and in the immediately adjacent Glen Lyon. There, Stewart (1969) plotted a large number of so called 'ring forts', arguing that these should be regarded as homestead sites. They are now so classified in the National Monuments Record. Their apparent scarcity along Loch Tay might be ascribed to different methods of working the land, obliterating traces there; but this seems unlikely because of their substantial nature. In Glen Lyon, she noted an association between 'ring forts' and areas of good pasture. The complementary map distributions of these and the crannogs might

76

thus indicate complementary functions, with the one being associated principally with pastoral and the other with arable land-use. But each may have had the comprehensive range of mixed-farming functions that Oakbank, with its byre and cereals, suggests was characteristic of at least some of the crannogs. Then the 'ring forts' may be sparsely represented by the loch side because there crannogs were preferred for essentially the same role.

The sites submerged in Tay and other lochs preserve organic materials that will yield much direct evidence on crannog economies to future excavators. However, because of the limited preservation of many dry-land sites, it seems likely that we may always be forced to rely heavily on interpretation of distribution maps in attempting to assess relationships between crannogs and sites such as 'ring forts' and duns. Such stone-built land sites are often more eye-catching elements in present-day landscapes than the crannogs, but because they are commonly short of small finds and preserved organic material, there is seldom much hope of further direct evidence on their dates or their precise functions.

One is also often reduced to analysis of map distributions in investigating relationships between settlement sites and land divisions or field patterns. Since fields and settlements are characteristically segregated from each other in the landscape, they tend not to build up overlapping stratigraphy, which might have been directly diagnostic of association. Nevertheless, over the last decade, it has become increasingly apparent in many parts of Britain that elements of land division may have very long lineages indeed (e.g. Fowler 1983, Mercer ed. 1981, Reeves-Smyth and Hamond eds 1983). As already noted, crannogs have unusual potential for distribution studies; because of their watery setting, there is a possibility of securing something approaching a 'total cull' of their pattern in the landscape. An initial study of the archaeological, documentary and cartographic evidence for Loch Tay has revealed patterns that are sufficiently intriguing to encourage further work on the theme of continuity in the landscape, there and elsewhere.

As their radiocarbon dates indicate, some at least of the Tay crannogs originated in the prehistoric period. Hints survive in charters and tacks that some were still being used in various ways into post-medieval times. Whilst many of the present-day land divisions reflect relatively recent developments, surveys made when the Breadalbane estates were re-organised in the eighteenth century document the pre-Improvement field system. Along the north side of the basin there is a considerable stretch of land of southerly exposure, with fairly good soils extending evenly along the lochside. This strip is suitable for cereal cropping, while the slopes above provide summer pastures. Remains on the ground and historical records show these upper and lower lands were worked in a system of complementary land use, involving the sheiling system of transhumance. Miller (1967) used Farquharson's 1769 survey to discuss the sheilings in relation to the pre-Improvement organisation of the cornlands beneath. With the regular altitudinal zonation of land-use potential, the land was organised in strips at right angles to the loch, so that each had a share of the different types of ground.

Miller was not concerned with crannog sites. What is interesting in the present context is that their disposition appears to correspond to a remarkable degree with the layout of the modules in the pre-Improvement land divisions. Where crannogs are absent, as at Loch Awe, this often corresponds with stretches where there is an abrupt drop-off close inshore. Otherwise, the even run of the lochside terrain allows considerable latitude in the placing of sites. Although some, such as *Eilean Breaban,* take advantage of local features such as the bedrock ridge there, it can not be argued that the overall grain of the terrain runs in such a way as to impose coinciding patterns on land divisions and the location of the crannogs. Since neither distribution appears closely determined in physiographic terms, their degree of coincidence suggests that a common human factor should be considered.

Many of the crannog mounds are now under water for much of the year. Nevertheless, it might be argued that their relationship to the field pattern might reflect merely their use as markers for march boundaries in a late division of the land, long after they themselves had been abandoned. This seems unlikely, however, since they tend to lie within the modules rather than defining their points of junction.

Many problems and imponderables remain, in this and in other cases, but it seems that we should at least entertain the possibility that we are faced by more than mere coincidence. The idea that we might be able to recover elements of the human organisation of Late Bronze Age or Iron Age landscapes is certainly more acceptable to the

4.7
8, 3.5

78

Figure 4.7 >

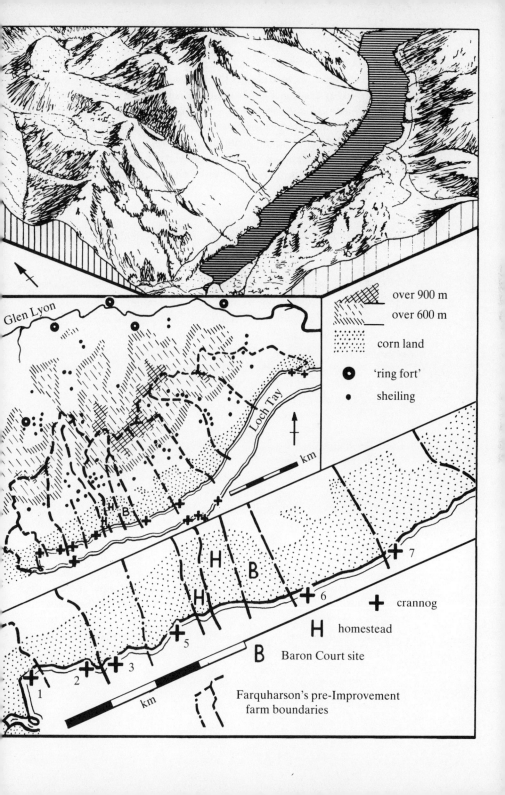

Glen Lyon

Loch Tay

over 900 m
over 600 m
corn land
'ring fort'
sheiling

km

+ crannog

H homestead

B Baron Court site

Farquharson's pre-Improvement
farm boundaries

km

archaeological community than it once seemed. We now know too that in Scotland, as in Ireland, the use of built-up islets has been one of the most persistent elements in the rural scene. With their possibilities for unusually complete distribution mapping on the one hand, and their preservation of organic indicators of their economic role on the other, they offer keys to interesting doors.

In Part Two, we shall consider some of the practical problems in carrying forward the investigation of these sites and their environmental relationships.

5. On Techniques of Investigation

A century after Munro we find ourselves asking a wider range of questions than earlier investigators of crannogs, and this at a time when resources for archaeology are limited. However, we have the advantage of techniques not accessible to our predecessors, and it is worth considering these in some detail because the work of recent years has shown how much scope there is for fieldwork. One aim of the present book is to encourage others to join in. Emphasis is laid on the use of modern diving gear, since this is the aspect of the research least familiar to most archaeologists. Because other methods, which have become common practice in modern archaeology and geomorphology, are treated in lesser detail there is some danger of losing sight of the value of applying these, too, to the study of crannogs. Diving is integral to the approach now adopted in Scotland, but it is only one element in co-ordinated research also involving work from the air and on the ground. That said, underwater work looms sufficiently large in the methodology to merit special attention here.

GENERAL CONSIDERATIONS. As Odo Blundell found in Edwardian times, the study of crannogs is severely hampered if one does not dive. Exposed portions of sites are generally less informative than submerged parts, where timbers and middens are protected from weathering and vandalism. Little is accomplished merely by peering through a glass-bottomed bucket. Blundell did well with the cumbersome diving equipment then available; with modern gear, it is much easier for archaeologists to become competent to pursue their research personally underwater. Submerged sites need not be left to commercial or sports divers, whose training is primarily in diving *per se* rather than in the academic discipline of archaeology.

The very ease, however, with which modern equipment allows one to work professionally underwater brings with it an insidious danger. For recreational divers, each dive is a special event. But for a research

81

worker, diving can become merely a mundane means towards the academic end. As one adapts to regular working days in the water, concentration can shift too completely to the gradually unfolding archaeology. As with pilots, familiarity may lead to an underestimation of an environment that remains essentially unforgiving, and can suddenly prove so (Welch 1978). Diving archaeologists have died in British waters, one while visiting a crannog. Working in the sheltered shallows of an inland lake can enhance a false sense of security, but lake water can be more lethal than sea water. Taken into the lung it passes more rapidly into the blood by osmosis, so drowning is faster. And though, chemically, the lochs may favour preservation of antiquities, they are less antiseptic than salt water. Even in the Highlands, far from industrial pollution, divers are troubled by bacterial inner-ear infections. In 1983 a child died from a lung infection contracted by inhaling loch water. Thus, although it is now relatively easy and inexpensive for researchers to go underwater to investigate crannogs, their attitude to diving should be just as professional as their involvement in archaeology. The Health and Safety Executive's *Diving Operations at Work Regulations* bear on archaeological diving (e.g. Croome 1981), and anyone contemplating work in British waters should check their current legal status with the Executive at Baynards House, Chepstow Place, London WC2.

In operational terms, however, compared to deep-sea work, diving on crannogs is neither complex nor expensive. Their very shallow depth means that almost all the work is done at ambient pressures of less than one additional atmosphere, so problems of narcosis and decompression do not arise, and compressed air consumption is minimal. Enough precharged cylinders can be carried in a car for a useful day of reconnaissance. For more protracted work, a small low-pressure compressor can supply several divers directly, *via* air hoses from shore or boat (the Nargile or Hookah system). This is the most cost-effective system for excavation, since work can continue for hour after hour, without periodic recharging of cylinders.

The main limitation on working time is water temperature. The bigger lochs contain several cubic kilometres of water, often fed by snow melt. In scheduling fieldwork, it pays to allow for temperature lag, avoiding spring when large bodies of water are at their coldest. For search and survey, where mobility is at a premium and the diver keeps

23, 24

82

warm through being on the move, there is much to be said for neo-
prene wet-suits (old hands ensure that the wetness inside the suit is
warm ; a tepid kettle is the politest but not the only recourse . . .). Excavation, however, entails lying static on the loch bed for long periods,
and then a dry-suit is very desirable. The hardy or impecunious wear
jerseys under wet-suits, with anoraks on top. The Oakbank excavation
demonstrated that six-hour days may in fact be worked underwater
with little more discomfort than is accepted on some British 'dry-land'
digs.

Let us now look at various aspects of the research in turn.

DISTRIBUTION MAPPING. The emancipation of excavations from reliance on casual drainage operations is not the only benefit that modern diving techniques bring to the study of crannogs. Diving searches
and non-disturbance surveys also have special value, since many lochs
seem likely to have retained most or even all of their original complement of crannog sites. Many of these are now wholly submerged, but
searches pursued with a combination of air, surface and underwater
techniques allow one to aim for something approaching a 'total cull' of
their remains. It is this that gives the unusual opportunity for meaningful studies of their distribution in the landscape.

Several layers of filters come between us and the actuality that was
the past. There is the propensity of sites of different kinds to survive in
different conditions. In certain areas, particular types may simply
deteriorate and vanish, or may tend to be destroyed by later activities.
But then material that actually survives may not be detected, or may
not enter the archaeological record. Preservation and perception are
not necessarily the same. Crannogs form an extreme example, in that
the covering of water that often preserves them so well has led to their
neglect relative to many potentially less-informative but more-visible
types of sites on shore.

Systematic mapping is only now getting under way with the availability of modern diving gear. Distribution maps based on the older
literature thus have serious limitations, reflecting the exigencies of discovery and reporting (cf. Hodder and Orton 1976). As we have seen,
the overall impression they give is conditioned by the incidence of
eighteenth- and nineteenth-century drainage work ; the apparent concentration in the south-west of Scotland owes much to Munro's activi-

ties; and the pattern in the Highlands to Blundell. However, crannog distributions established by systematic searches with modern techniques have the potential of avoiding some of the problems intrinsic to distribution maps of many categories of land sites: for example the tendency for the patterns of the past to be erased in the areas of the best land, because of the intensity of later activities there. One would need a very special reason to trouble to dredge up old crannogs from loch beds. Some were indeed demolished, either in the period of use, on military grounds (e.g. in Loch Lochy); or later, as in Loch Tay, where one impeded the access of Victorian steamers to a jetty: but even there the debris remains. Islets were certainly reworked, but in Scotland there seem to have been few cases where they may have been entirely obliterated or overlaid by unrelated later activities (as is happening to some of the Swiss submerged lake-side settlements, with land reclamation and marina development). Though the dating of lake-level changes can be problematic, it is generally feasible in each loch basin to make a geomorphological assessment of the possibility of changes of sufficient magnitude to have affected the survival of sites.

Compared to the palimpsest of overlying landscapes on shore, many lochs thus afford us a fair chance of recovering a distribution pattern that is complete enough to offer insights into the location of sites, both in relation to the features of the lochs themselves, and to the surrounding landscape. The interest of this type of 'total cull' approach has been demonstrated by Renfrew and others, first in Malta (Renfrew 1973, Renfrew and Level 1979) and then in Orkney (e.g. Davidson in Renfrew 1979). They looked at dry-land sites that were so massive as to suggest that a total pattern might be retrieved, because of the unlikelihood of destruction without trace. But those were major tombs and specialised ritual structures: crannogs were elements in the everyday life of their users.

SEARCH PROCEDURES. If this unusual opportunity to study the distribution patterns of domestic structures is to be exploited, effective search techniques are required. Many of the larger lochs cover tens of square kilometres. With so many sites totally submerged, and sub-surface visibility seldom more than 10 metres, it is clearly impracticable for divers to search their whole area. Happily this is not necessary.

The bathymetrical charts made under the direction of Sir John Murray, the distinguished oceanographer of the Challenger expedition (Murray and Pullar 1910 *et seq.*), provide outstanding assistance. These depict the bottom topography of no less than 562 Scottish lochs. 60000 soundings are mapped at their surveyed positions, so the distinction between interpolation and hard data is clear, and large segments of the lochs can be eliminated immediately as being much too deep for crannog building. The shallow areas so identified may then be searched from the air, either directly or by using photographs. Even fully submerged crannogs often show up well. From low altitude one *5, 6, 8* may pick up underwater details such as breakwater foundations, not readily seen from a boat. Indeed such patterns can be difficult for a swimmer to make out while actually crawling around their boulders. But low flying presents problems in Highland glens. Their narrow steep-sided forms and wind-shears discourage the orbiting of sites. Use is therefore made of the national collections of vertical air photo cover. Much of this is at 1 : 10000 scale. This is too small for detail, but its hyper-stereoscopic view of the topography of the shallows allows likely mounds to be located for evaluation by diving.

It is difficult to eliminate the possibility that some unobtrusive or wholly mud-buried crannogs may be missed, but systematic application of these procedures can at least make distribution maps much less haphazard, while reducing the search task to economically manageable proportions. In the survey of Loch Awe, for example, by combining these approaches, the fieldwork problem was reduced from that of a blind search of some 90 km of shoreline to a specific investigation, by diving, of some sixty mounds at known locations. One in three of these proved to be artificially built-up.

Experiments carried out by Professor Harold Edgerton of M.I.T. and the writer showed that side-scan sonar can be effective in searching Scottish lochs for crannogs and other man-made features, as well as for portraying their details. One should not, however, neglect 'low-technology' approaches, including that traditional tactic of archaeological fieldworkers (cf. Coles 1984), the visit to the local pub. Information from 'the regulars' is often valuable, even when they have not themselves recognised crannogs. In areas of featureless or muddy loch bed, fish like to lie in the shelter of stony mounds. Anglers and ghillies know their positions well. Indeed an iron fish on top of a stake can well indicate that a crannog lies beneath, as at Mary's Distaff in Loch Tay.

85

INITIAL EVALUATION OF SITES. Participants in the initial surveys of Loch Awe and Loch Tay agreed not to disturb sites or their surrounding stratigraphy. It was recognised that this policy would disallow some cases where limited excavation might readily have secured corroboration that mounds were crannogs. Nevertheless, it was felt that the ethical and practical disadvantages of a proliferation of trial pits outweighed this. With so many potential sites now readily accessible to divers, it seems desirable to encourage others also to hold to this non-destructive principle, and to resist the temptations of haphazard digging.

Just as most hillforts are distinguishable without excavation from natural features, so too with crannogs. In geomorphological terms, the shapes and locations of many mounds would be difficult to account for by any natural process, quite apart from positive artificial features that confirm them to be crannogs. Sometimes a mound is made up of quite different material from the lake bed around it; e.g. a rock pile may stand upon silt. Indeed stone size in itself can offer a clue. Although for different structural purposes crannog builders used everything from rocks of over a ton down to gravel, the visible parts of most confirmed crannogs appear to consist mainly of medium-sized stones: big enough not to wash out, but small enough for a man to handle without risking a hernia.

Whilst such clues as these may be apparent from above the surface, they hardly constitute primary proof. Diving is therefore used as a matter of routine to search for diagnostic details and check their credibility. There is no substitute for close first-hand scrutiny of the layout of features or the provenance of finds on the lake bed. Patterns of stones may indicate causeways, jetties, or canoe-docks. Timbers may show organised relationships, and signs of carpentry (such as mortice joints). Random waterlogged wood tends to accumulate around mounds, however, and some worked timbers have proved to be drifted components from old jetties and disintegrated boats. Midden deposits are visible at the foot of some mounds, while durable artifacts like querns may be found lying exposed. Quite apart from their role in the making of duty-free whisky, portable objects such as these must always be regarded with circumspection, since they make handy anchors for fishermen (like the superannuated sewing-machines also found on crannogs). Thus a single find or feature of a mound should seldom be

Plate 16. *Oakbank* crannog: internal structural timbers, 10-20 cm diameter.

Plate 17. Eroded gangway piles protruding from lake bed, off *Oakbank*.

Plate 18. Side-scan sonar image of *Cherry Island* crannog, Loch Ness, showing submerged breakwater.

Plate 19. Side-scan sonar, *Lochend,* Loch Ness. Artificial, but not crannogs: circular spoil heaps from Telford's early steam dredger.

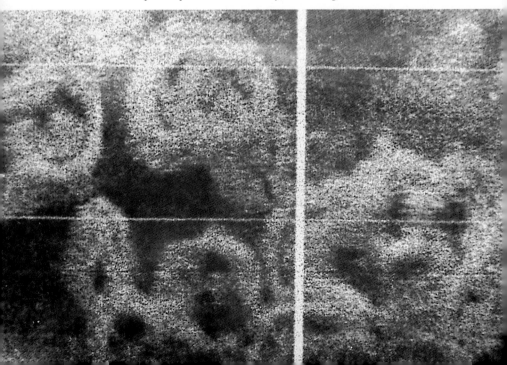

Plate 20. Radial survey of a Loch Awe crannog, with tape and sounding rod.

Plate 21. Distomat, ranging on prism target positioned by diver in Loch Tay.

Plate 22. Small finds being written-up on site, then bagged and pegged to a collection tray.

accepted as a definite indication that it is a crannog. What one looks for in an initial evaluation is a combination of characteristics sufficiently comprehensive to render other explanations unlikely. Perhaps the safest evidence obtainable without recourse to excavation is the existence of arrays of piles, surrounding a mound and perhaps delineating *17, 24* a gangway that linked it to the shore. It may, however, take determined searching to find them. They have often rotted off flush with the lake bed, and their tops may be camouflaged by mud. The use of the word 'causeway' in the literature is unfortunate, in that it leads people to expect substantial features in stone, rather than encouraging them to search for these more subtle traces.

MORPHOLOGICAL SURVEY. On land, it is often possible to appreciate the layout of a site by simply walking over it, without the need of measured surveys. With crannogs, however, surveying can seldom be avoided. It is not only a matter of 'making the invisible visible' for non-diving colleagues. The diver has problems of perception too. Although diving can not be rivalled for close inspection of detail, limitations on visibility stand in the way of a wider view of the site. Algal blooms set off by agricultural chemicals in Lowland lochs, or the peatiness of Highland waters, can sometimes give the impression of swimming through pea soup or black coffee. But even in pellucid water the shallowness of crannog tops usually prevents an overview of the plan, even when one can swim right across the site. Perversely, crannogs still visible above the surface as islands often present the greatest difficulties in appreciating layout. Protected from grazing animals, their exposed parts are often thickly overgrown. It is easy to miss systematic stone patterns while stumbling through brambly brush or amongst half-awash boulders. Early on in our work it became clear that it would be necessary to develop recording procedures that could be applied consistently from site to site, if comparisons were to be meaningful. Since, at the present stage of research, the more teams that can be encouraged to undertake primary survey work the better, it seems worth outlining some of the practices developed.

BASIC RECORDING TECHNIQUES. A distinction can be made between the degree of precision desirable in controlling the details of an individual excavation, and the less stringent requirements for a basic

87

inventory of previously unrecorded sites. Furthermore, in dealing with partly collapsed structures, there is little point at the reconnaissance stage in putting the limited resources available into drawing every stone of a very few sites. In the present state of knowledge, it seems more useful to record a larger number of sites in a relatively simple but consistent fashion: that is, to secure basic but dependable portraits of these otherwise largely invisible antiquities. It is necessary to establish their degree of variability, by documenting their size range, their characteristic shapes and types of appendages, and their relationships to the terrain.

'High' and 'low' technology approaches to surveying have both proved of value. For example, by using the ultrasonic frequency range, sonar effectively avoids the problems of light-based underwater survey systems. Experiments by Professor H. A. Edgerton and the writer have shown that, even in very shallow water, high-resolution side-scan sonar can delineate the underwater shapes of crannogs. It only took a few minutes to secure the imagery of Cherry Island in Loch Ness, where Odo Blundell had dived at the turn of the century, but this revealed features, such as a submerged breakwater, that do not figure in the museum model of that crannog.

Approaches to amphibious survey using much less expensive equipment have also proved effective. One such involves working from the centre of the crannog, measuring bearings by waterproof compass or yachtsman's plastic sextant, and distances by fibreglass tape. At least eight radial sections are measured across the mound and out over the neighbouring lake bed, to document its shape and relationship to the underwater topography. Denser measurements are made to depict special features such as docks. Measurement points are identified by a diver, who also takes depth readings with a sounding staff (merely a plastic drainpipe calibrated with insulating tape). If the water is too deep for this, a tape is used as a lead-line, and the work is done from an inflatable dinghy controlled by a kedge anchor laid out along the radius under measurement. The surface of the loch is used as local datum, and its level during the survey is tied in to an Ordnance Survey benchmark on shore. Any parts protruding above the surface are levelled with a waterproof Suunto clinometer. Details of timbers and finds are added by tape trilateration.

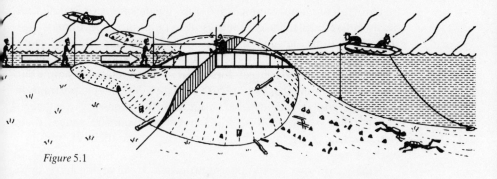

Figure 5.1

CONTROL SURVEY FOR EXCAVATION. A higher order of precision is required of survey measurements intended to control a dig; that is, to provide a reliable skeleton for the detailed recording, and to tie in the relationships of different excavation areas in three dimensions. When excavating deepwater sites such as shipwrecks, the only practical course is to do all survey control work directly on the sea bed. Some excavators in the shallows of Swiss and French lakes have also chosen to survey entirely beneath the surface. Bocquet (1979) has an elegant system based on taping interlocking equilateral triangles. Laying-in accurate control by tape under water can be difficult, however, particularly when the breaks of slope of a crannog mound are involved. Low visibility makes it hard to maintain alignments accurately, or to co-ordinate work between divers without voice communication. Even a slight current makes tapes billow. Ultrasonic underwater range-finders are not yet widely accessible, whereas powerful land-based surveying instruments may be borrowed from normal academic sources. At Oakbank the writer therefore decided to work through the air/water interface, using tacheometry from the shore.

The instrument used was a Wild Distomat (a theodolite fitted with an infrared rangefinder and microprocessor). This combined speed of 5.2 operation with a useful degree of precision (Morrison 1980b). It was aimed at a prism target on an extended staff placed on measuring *21* points by a diver, and kept vertical by spirit level. Measurements of positions on the crannog and the surrounding lake bed could be replicated to within 5 cm. This was considered adequate for illustrating the relationship to the site of the metal control framework for the dig. Accuracy of this order made it easy to plot the detailed morphology of

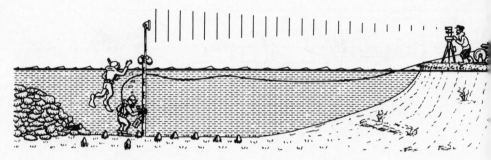

Figure 5.2

the site and its outlying features, since the positions of closely juxtaposed piles, say, could be reliably resolved. The points to be measured
were selected and numbered in advance, and the diver with the staff
followed a sketch-map, of which the Distomat operator had a copy. A
snorkeller provided liaison between them by a simple code of hand
signals. In areas of dense detail, where the diver did not have to walk
far between points, it proved possible to average one observation
every couple of minutes.

RECORDING EXCAVATED DETAIL. The metal frame, positioned *via*
control points located by the tacheometric survey, gave the divers
their immediate three-dimensional reference for the detailed recording of the dig. A variety of methods are available for plotting detail
within such a reference system.

As on land, trilateration is more reliable than taping off-sets with
estimated right-angles. It can be fast as well as accurate if twin tapes
are used with a trilateration graticule on the drawing-board. This
system has the advantage of allowing the excavator to plan without an
assistant, and the writer has found it useful on dry-land sites too,
though he devised it originally to get round the problems of communicating whilst submerged. For underwater use, a re-usable graticule is
5.3   drawn on plastic draughting film with etching ink. The underwater
plotting is done with soft pencil, to be erased when the plan has been
traced off.

Areas of complex detail in plans or sections can also be drawn in the
usual way, with the help of a frame divided into, say, 20-cm squares.

90

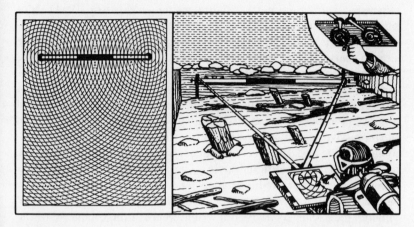

Figure 5.3

Sometimes, rather than make reduced drawings on site, it is convenient to record at 1:1, and then to do the reductions at leisure on shore. A metre square of rigid clear plastic sheet is positioned according to the site grid over the segment or section to be recorded, and details are traced off life-size, using wax crayons. Ashore, the sheet is laid over a scale grid, and the drawing either copied off manually or photographed, while the diver is working on the next sheet. As Dr Ruoff's team have also found, problems of parallax in working with grids or transparencies can be overcome by using plumb bobs or simple sighting devices.

The instantaneous and comprehensive record that photography offers can be of great value. On excavation, artifacts and remains of vegetation often retain much of their natural colour, but this can fade within minutes. Site photography underwater is occasionally impracticable because of muddiness or algae, and low light levels and lack of contrast are always major problems. Modern high-speed colour films *7, 14* and underwater flash units can, however, be used to advantage, since *16, 17* suspended particulate matter is not a problem in many of the Scottish lochs. The blackness of their waters is due largely to peat dye; so though attenuation of light is severe, back-scatter is not serious and it is profitable to use powerful strobes (Morrison 1978b). Photography can assist planning in various ways, without necessarily requiring

91

expensive photogrammetric equipment (e.g. Morrison 1969). Mosaics and stereo pairs offer approaches to recording and communicating the three-dimensional complexity characteristic within these sites, because of their remarkable preservation of organic materials.

As one visitor put it, viewing ranks of upright timbers at Oakbank, *7, 10, 16* 'on land sites we have post-holes; here you've got the posts . . .' Whilst not yet rivalling the 9-m pile found protruding 4 m from the lake bed at Fiavè (Perini 1976), timbers encountered in Scottish sites are often of impressive length. The survival of striking three-dimensional remains in these and other wetland sites raises the whole question of the adequacy of the traditional style of archaeological planning. It is accepted that what remains of many land sites can be portrayed quite satisfactorily by one or more plan views, with a limited number of spot heights, plus some sections. But crannogs are at the other end of the spectrum from, say, some dry-land sites on gravel terraces, which time has reduced essentially to two dimensions. Instead, one is confronted by upstanding but partially collapsed composite wood-and-stone structures, with some elements that were perhaps originally installed at oblique angles for structural reasons. A credible analysis depends on provision being made for an effective record of the azimuth and steepness of their orientations. Standard orthographic drawings have limitations as tools for interpreting such data. Both computer modelling and physical model-building are being used effectively on similar problems in analysing the forms and construction of ancient ships, notably by Richard Steffy. The writer has accordingly been experimenting with both an interactive graphics system on a microcomputer and a mechanical analogue Perspektomat, while Dr Dixon has used a hardware model to clarify the interpretation of the Oakbank dig. Such techniques serve as tools of exposition as well as research, and were used in developing perspective views for this book.

EXCAVATION. Computer techniques are desirable, not only for analysing spatial organisation, but also as database systems for coping with the intricacy and sheer volume of the data that confronts one when a crannog is opened up. It might be argued that the real problem of excavating these sites lies not so much in their being underwater, as in their characteristic combination of complexity with vulnerability. This they have in common with many wetland sites, with equally well-preserved organic structures and debris. It is no easy matter to excavate such sites in air, working amid glutinous material that may compact under its own weight if the water table is lowered (and which can certainly be damaged by ponderous archaeologists, let alone wheelbarrows). These sites deteriorate disastrously if allowed to dry out, and often have to be kept sprayed while under excavation. Professor Coles has recently suggested it would be logical to build a cofferdam round a terrestrial wetland site, not with the intention of draining it but, rather, 'completely flooding it, and then excavating it under water. Problems of keeping the site damp, of lifting artifacts, and of keeping the excavators off the site, would all be solved' (1984, 48). This will hardly be greeted with enthusiasm by dry academics, but the idea has its appeal to those who have attempted to excavate two-thousand-year-old hurdling and straw ropes, found under half-ton boulders, amid timbers as large as telegraph poles but with the strength *14, 16* of carrots. The technical success of Dr Dixon's Oakbank dig has confirmed that underwater excavation of crannogs is justified not only because it allows the selection of a site on academic grounds, free from the exigencies of casual drainage, but also because it has demonstrated that the advantages sought by Coles are indeed attainable, even on a small budget.

When confronted with such richly preserved intricacy, those who took part at Oakbank agreed that they would not like to have had to cope with the problems of working 'between wind and water', as earlier excavators of crannogs had perforce to do. As one bemused excavator fresh from a drier dig in Syria put it, a crannog mound is something like a wet *tel*, with all the problems of sorting out rebuilding *5.4* phases, and recognising later construction elements that come down from above, to pierce through earlier deposits and structures. The potential of site-specific tree-ring studies for matching components that belong to the same phase will clearly have to be developed. The Swiss use a computer database so that each day's findings can shape the next day's excavation strategy (Ruoff, pers. comm.).

Although crannog excavators certainly have to embrace some entirely new procedures, the actual mechanics of excavation are often familiar. Visitors to the Oakbank dig were often more intrigued by the way that the customary trowels, tapes and snap-top bags were used on the loch bed, than by the strange paraphernalia of the divers. This

Figure 5.4. The notion of a wet *tel*, combining multiple ancient phases
and recent legacies.

reflects the approach of those chiefly involved, whose background
leads them to regard this work as an extension of the discipline of
archaeology they practice on land, that is, merely archaeology that
happens to lie underwater, rather than something separate entitled
'Underwater Archaeology'. Thus, while seeking to develop practices
that come to sensible terms with the specific working environment, the
aim has been to maintain the standards of modern above-surface
practice. Underwater, it has proved feasible to excavate in fully controlled trenches, maintaining normal sections and using versions of
many of the usual dig methods.

    Modifications are often very simple. Trowels and spatulae are sup-
plemented for delicate work by finning with the hand. Trench-notes
and labels are written on plastic foil with an ordinary pencil, and spring
clothes-pegs stop bagged small finds from drifting away. As mud is
stirred up, visibility is maintained by a pump that provides a moving
curtain of clean water *via* a perforated tube (known as the Magic
Flute, from its warbling). Water-jet devices are also used to provide
controlled suction, to remove light spoil. Shifting heavy weights is
much easier than wrestling a wheelbarrow across slippery planks on
land. No stress need be put on vulnerable organic matter or fragile
structures when overlying boulders are lifted off by the controlled
inflation of an air-bag, and a boat with a tray underneath can serve as
a dumper truck. Since the average density of rocks is only about two
and a half times that of water, immersion produces a very significant

22

5.5

Figure 5.5

reduction in their effective weight, to the benefit of the excavators as well as the original builders of the crannogs. The diggers can ballast themselves to hover comfortably while working on delicate parts of the site, a point appreciated by those who have had to lie on duckboards suspended over wetland sites ashore for days on end.

The freedom in space of the diver compared to the earth-bound excavator does not, however, solve all of the problems posed by the quality of survival of organic material. On dry-land sites, we seldom have the problem of having too short a reach to dig down through arrays of close-set fragile posts, standing higher than one's arm is long. One may be faced with razing parts of the crannog's structures before one fully understands them, in order to get at the lower parts where the answers may lie. The richness of crannog sites in non-structural organic materials also presents problems. Whereas on some land sites, one may feel lucky to recover a trace of organic debris from a posthole, on crannogs there are often literally cubic metres to cope with. These can range from domestic middens and the waste from craft processes, to byre deposits a metre or more thick. The practical aspects of securing samples underwater present no insurmountable problems. As Dr Dixon has demonstrated, columns can be cut and boxed; cores lodged in plastic drainpipes; and slurry drawn off in syringes. It is the methodological issues in sampling strategy that present the real difficulties. As is so often the case in archaeology, it is not always obvious how ethical ideals and economic realities may best be reconciled.

SAMPLING AND CONSERVATION. It is not feasible to conserve and retain all the products of a crannog excavation. In a very real sense the whole site is an artifact. Small ones contain tens, and larger ones hundreds, of tons of material that would not have got there but for human agency. This has been apparent from the very start of archaeological investigations. Before Wilde began his seminal examination of Lagore crannog in Ireland in 1839, some 150 cartloads of bones had been mined from the site and shipped to Scotland as manure. With neither incentive nor technology for investigating and conserving organic material, the early excavators simply had their workmen shovel it aside.

Occasionally they expressed regret when artifacts disintegrated. A passage from the Lochlee (Ayrshire) work of 1878 sums up what happened on even the better conducted early digs:

. . . 5 feet deep, the workmen discovered, amongst decayed brushwood and chips of wood, a beautiful trough cut out of a single block of wood. It was quite whole when found, and showed very distinctly the markings of the gouge-like instrument by which it was fashioned. It was made of soft wood, which, upon drying, quickly crumbled into dust . . . (in Munro 1882, 93)

5.6   Nothing more specific is reported of the nature of the woods and
7, 15 brushwood; we are lucky that an engraving of the general form of that artifact survives, though it does not show the tool marks.

Nowadays, fairly effective conservation techniques are available, but at a price. In deciding preservation priorities within limited budgets, exhibitable artifacts will understandably attract most museum support. This can be justified not only because of their role in com-

96

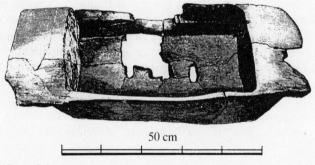

50 cm

Figure 5.6

municating with the public, but because the wide range of functional and decorative articles preserved on crannogs can give insights into everyday life on contemporary land sites, where similar objects must often be presumed though they may not have survived.

Between 'environmental data' and 'exhibitable objects' there is a class of material that requires special consideration, not only in crannogs but in many other wetland sites. This is that of 'used wood'. Much of the material found on the sites, from tree trunks down to twigs, in itself would hardly be accepted by a museum as 'an artifact'. Many pieces show little or no sign of working. Yet they were all brought there originally for a purpose, and effort had been expended in obtaining them. It is not adequate merely to record their structural relationships and stratigraphy, and then to discard them. Information is not only to be gained from their organisation within the mound. In themselves they can offer evidence on a range of topics. Cut marks can give the clue to tools that have not themselves survived, but if the original three-dimensional organic object is not available for study a specialist is seriously limited in what he may conclude at second hand from ordinary drawings and photographs. Neither should tool-marks be the only criterion of selection. It is already clear that standard lengths and diameters, straightness and absence of knots can indicate managed woodlands, and techniques such as pollarding. It is desirable that representative material from excavated contexts should be retained, for further study as more subtle means of diagnosis are developed.

97

In Part One of the book, it was suggested that a large number of questions had still to be answered regarding crannogs. The work of recent years has confirmed the promise suggested by the early reports, and has shown that techniques for realising that potential are no longer lacking. The main problem is now the definition of priorities, relative to the management of limited research resources.

Conclusion

'. . . some of the obscurest antiquities of Scotland . . .'
George Chalmers (1813)

Much more is certainly known about crannogs now than when Chalmers, author of the antiquarian treatise *Caledonia,* commented that they were amongst the most obscure of his country's antiquities. Nevertheless, it remains true that compared to many other types of sites, they have received little scholarly attention relative to their potential for producing information. As we have seen, few have been excavated to anything approaching modern standards, and despite their persistence far into the period of historical records, documentary evidence is less helpful than might have been hoped. Even establishing a satisfactory definition appears rather less straightforward than it may once have seemed.

Information that has accrued since Chalmers's day on constructions in watery settings elsewhere in the world does, however, present opportunities for insights into the Scottish sites, by comparing motives and methods for using such specialised locations. Much is now known not only about the Alpine lake sites, but about artificial islets of contrasting scale and organisation from the North Sea basin to the Shatt al Arab or indeed Oceania. Strangely enough, some of the closest parallels for the Scottish sites are to be found farthest off, in New Zealand, where the Maoris used both built-up islets and hill forts right up to the lifetime of Robert Munro. There are obvious perils in over-enthusiastic pursuit of ethnographic parallels (e.g. Hodder 1982), but the sheer variety of environments and cultures with built-up islets insures against a blinkered use of analogy, and their very diversity helps to bring out those factors that are indeed common denominators in small-island life.

In evidence from elsewhere, and from within Scotland itself, a recurrent theme is apparent. Island-builders may have sought isolation, but their products can not be regarded *in* isolation. Their use of

99

the islets was part of life in the landscapes that formed their setting, and generally seems to have been interwoven with it in a whole range of ways, direct and indirect. Even those cases where links seem minimal appear to be best understood as negative reactions against aspects of life on shore.

It would therefore seem a great shame if future crannog studies were regarded as anything other than an integral part of archaeology as a whole. It would be particularly unfortunate if they were seen as something divorced from the rest of the discipline, merely because of the necessity of special techniques of access. We now know that with modern underwater gear archaeologists can themselves work effectively on these sites, so investigations need not be left to those whose prime interest is in diving *per se*. Equally, while the problems of defining a crannog may be interesting, they should not be allowed to circumscribe future research. As suggested above, it would seem counter-productive to constrain this within a narrow definition designed to separate crannogs from, say, sites set on natural islets. As their promiscuous use of unspecialised words for *island* indicates, those who actually used the sites do not seem to have been greatly concerned with classifying their manner of genesis. Indeed, one may suspect that some who re-used long-abandoned artificial islets may have neither known nor cared that they were originally man-made. The dominant impression one gains from studying the sites in the field is of pragmatism, with the users taking advantage of whatever natural or previously-built features would serve their purposes. This seems to hold true of choices not only in the water, but between shore and water. Both locally, within individual loch basins, and over a broader regional view of Scotland, the indications are of decisions being made between islets and shore sites, such as duns, in terms of shrewd assessments of topography and available materials. There would seem to be much to be said for taking an holistic view, and considering the study of the environmental, economic and settlement information that crannogs can yield as an extension of the study of the landscape into the water, rather than as something to set apart from the rest of archaeology.

We have seen that crannogs can be of especial interest in landscape studies, because their tendency to survive under water can offer prospects for mapping something approaching a complete regional distribution, not overwritten by later activities. There is a great deal of scope in Scotland for further amphibious search and survey operations, and the work already done shows that amateur groups, using inexpensive techniques of measurement, could accomplish much of genuine research value without disturbing or endangering sites in any way.

The chance of obtaining relatively complete distributions for many loch basins is one side of the unusual preservation of crannogs. It is an aspect that may be exploited in a straightforward way, and one can unreservedly support the idea of extensive future campaigns of non-destructive surveys. The other side, their high standard of internal preservation of organic materials, is a more complex blessing. In terms of environmental and economic evidence, the crannog sites have a potential for eloquent testimony that contrasts markedly with the stony recalcitrance characteristic of so many duns and brochs on land. But their very richness is in itself a problem. With information to offer at all levels from pollen grains, *via* beetles and straw chaff, up to oak trunk structures weighing tons, it is clear that the digging of a crannog is but the first step in its analysis. It is not something to undertake lightly, because of the scale of the commitment to post-excavation work. In this, crannogs share in the economic and ethical dilemma that the current growth of interest in wetland sites in general poses for the limited resources of archaeology as a whole.

To a greater extent than ever before, we are aware of the information potential of macro- and micro-scopic organic remains. The rate of progress in recent decades in developing investigative techniques has, however, underlined that our own efforts will not be definitive. The casual shovelling aside of what we now perceive as environmental data, and the crumbling to dust of wooden artifacts, so often described by earlier excavators, may now excite righteous disapproval. But this is pointless unless we in turn acknowledge a responsibility to preserve material from the sites that we disturb, so that it may be subjected to more advanced appraisal in the future. Even the microscopic parasites in the dung of byre deposits can prove indicators of the intensity with which pasture was used, giving clues to land management methods. Though only a small percentage of the total environmental material present in major crannogs can be recovered and retained, thought ought to be given to developing sampling strategies that will make

101

flexible provision for work by our successors. This will surely include approaches unforseen by us.

A hundred years after Robert Munro's heyday, the study of the crannogs of Scotland has thus reached an intriguing stage. Old debates have been re-opened, new types of questions have been posed, and new responsibilities have been recognised. It has become apparent that through the use of modern diving techniques, work consistent with the standards of present-day professional archaeology may now be carried out economically underwater on these sites. This should free modern investigators from the dependence on casual drainage forced on their precursors, allowing more coherent research strategies to be developed. But there is a long way to go yet, and one can only hope that in a further century's time future researchers will feel that those of this generation did as well, in terms of the standards of their time, as did Robert Munro and Odo Blundell, the delving doctor and the diving priest.

Plate 23. Divers in dry- and wet-suits prepare to investigate a crannog as snow meltwater flows into Loch Tay.

Plate 24. Diver (wearing anorak for additional warmth) excavates delicately by fanning mud away with his hands.

Bibliography

Abbreviations
B A R = British Archaeological Reports
I J N A = International Journal of Nautical Archaeology
P S A S = Proceedings of the Society of Antiquaries of Scotland
RCAHMS = Royal Commission on the Ancient and Historical
Monuments of Scotland

Birks, H. (1977) The Flandrian forest history of Scotland: a preliminary synthesis, in Shotton, ed. (1977) pp.119-35.
Blundell, O. (1908-9) Notices of the examination by means of a diving dress of the artificial island or crannog of Eilean Muireach in the south end of Loch Ness. *PSAS 43*, 159-64.
——(1909-10) On further examination of artificial islands in the Beauly Firth, Loch Bruiach, Loch Moy, Loch Garry, Loch Lundy, Loch Oich, Loch Lochy, and Loch Treig. *PSAS 44*, 12-33.
——(1912-13) Further notes on the artificial islands in the Highland area. *PSAS 47*, 257-302.
Bocquet, A. (1979) Lake-Bottom Archaeology. *Sci. Amer. 240.2*, 48-56.
Borchgrevinck, A-B. (1980) The Houses of the Norwegian Seters. *Northern Studies 16*, 53-69.
Butzer, K. (1982) *Archaeology as Human Ecology*. Cambridge.
Caulfield, D. (1870) Account of an Expedition undertaken by Lord Deputy Sidney to attack a crannoge in a Lough near Omagh. *J. Roy. Hist. and Archaeol. Assoc. of Ireland 1* (4th series).
Childe, V. G. (1942) *What Happened in History*. London.
Clanranald (1819) *Historical and Genealogical Account of the Clan or Family of MacDonald . . . particularly . . . the Clan Ranald*. Edinburgh.
Clay, G. (1980) *Close-Up: How to read the American City*. Chicago.
Coles, J. (1984) *The Archaeology of Wetlands*. Edinburgh.

103

Collingwood, R. G. (1946) *The Idea of History.* Oxford.

Croome, A. (1981) New diving regulations. *IJNA 10.4,* 343.

Cunliffe, B. (1978) *Iron Age Communities in Britain,* 2nd edn. London.

—— & Rowley, T., eds (1978) Lowland Iron Age Communities in Europe. *BAR* S-48.

Diarmad (pseudonym) (1876) Oran na Comhachaig. *An Gaidheal 5,* 328-36.

Davidson, D. (1979) The Orcadian Environment and Cairn Location, in Renfrew (1979) 7-20.

Dixon, T. N. (1981) Radiocarbon dates for crannogs in Loch Tay. *IJNA 10.4,* 346-7.

——(1982) A survey of crannogs in Loch Tay. *PSAS 112,* 17-38.

——(1984) *Scottish Crannogs: Underwater excavation of artificial islands with special reference to Oakbank Crannog, Loch Tay.* Unpubl. PhD thesis, Univ. of Edinburgh.

Donaldson, G. (1974) *Scotland – the Shaping of a Nation.* Newton Abbot.

Drury, P., ed. (1982) *Structural Reconstruction. BAR* 110.

Dwelly, E. (1949) *The Illustrated Gaelic English Dictionary.* Glasgow.

Evans, J., Limbrey, S. & Cleere, H., eds (1975) *The Effect of Man on the Landscape: the Highland Zone.* CBA Research Report 11, London.

Fenton, A. (1968) Plough and Spade in Dumfries and Galloway. *Trans. Dumfries & Galloway N. H. & A. Soc. 45,* 147-88.

——(1972) The currach in Scotland, with notes on the floating of timber. *Scottish Studies 16,* 61-81.

Fojut, N. (1982) Towards a Geography of Shetland Brochs. *Glasgow Archaeol. J. 9,* 38-59.

Fowler, P. (1983) *The Farming of Prehistoric Britain.* Cambridge.

Fraser, H. (1917) Investigation of the Artificial Island in Loch Kinellan, Strathpeffer. *PSAS 51,* 48-98.

Gatrell, A. (1983) *Distance and Space: a Geographical Perspective.* Oxford.

Gilbert, J. (1979) *Hunting and Hunting Reserves in Medieval Scotland.* Edinburgh.

Gillies, W. (1938) *In Famed Breadalbane.* Perth.

Gordon, R. (1630) *History of the Earldom of Sutherland.* Edinburgh.

Graham, A. (1950-51) Archaeological gleanings from Dark Age
    records. *PSAS 85*, 64-91.
Grant, I. (1961) *Highland Folk Ways.* London.
Grose, F. (1797) *Antiquities of Scotland.* Edinburgh.
Guido, M. (1974) A Scottish crannog re-dated. *Antiquity 48,* 54-6.
Haldane, A. (1973) *The Drove Roads of Scotland.* Edinburgh.
Hanson, W. & Maxwell, G. (1983) *Rome's North West Frontier –
    the Antonine Wall.* Edinburgh.
Harding, A., ed. (1982) *Climatic Change in Later Prehistory.*
    Edinburgh.
Hardy, B., ed. (1973) *A report on the survey of Loch Awe for evidence
    of lake dwellings.* Naval Air Command S.A.C.
Hayes-McCoy, G. (1964) *Ulster and other Irish Maps c.1600.* Dublin.
Hodder, I. (1982) *The Present Past.* London.
—— & Orton, C. (1976) *Spatial Analysis in Archaeology.* Cambridge.
Ivens, W. (1930) *Island Builders of the Pacific.* London.
Jankuhn, H. (1977) *Einfürung in die Siedlungsarchäologie.* Berlin.
Joos, M. (1982) Swiss Midland Lakes and Climatic Changes, in
    Harding, A., ed. (1982).
Keller, F. (1866) (trans. J. Lee) *The Lake Dwellings of Switzerland
    and other parts of Europe.* London.
Lacy, B. (1983) *Archaeological Survey of County Donegal.* Lifford.
Laing, L. (1975) Settlement types in post-Roman Scotland. *BAR 13.*
McArdle, C. & D., & Morrison, I. (1973) Scottish Lake Dwelling
    Survey. *IJNA 2.2,* 381-2.
MacDonald, C. (1889) *Moidart, or Among the Clanranalds.* Oban.
Macdonald, G. (1932) Notes on the Roman Forts at Old Kilpatrick
    and Croy Hill. *PSAS 66,* 219-76.
Mackechnie, J. (1946) *The Owl of Strone.* Glasgow.
McNeill, P. & Nicholson, R. (1975) *An Historical Atlas of Scotland.*
    St Andrews.
Macpherson, N. (1878) Notes on the Antiquities from the Island of
    Eigg. *PSAS 12,* 577-97.
Mapleton, R. (1870) i: Notice of an Artificial Island in Loch
    Kielziebar; ii: Description of Stockaded Remains at Arisaig.
    PSAS 7, 322-4, 516-19.
Mercer, R., ed. (1981) *Farming Practice in British Prehistory.*
    Edinburgh.

Miller, R. (1967) Land Use by Summer Sheilings. *Scottish Studies 11.2*, 193-221.

Mitchell, A. (1880) *The Past in the Present.* Edinburgh.

——, ed. (1907) *Geographical Collections relating to Scotland made by Walter MacFarlane,* vol.2. Edinburgh.

Monteith, J. (1937) The crannog at Lochend, Coatbridge. *Trans. Glasgow Archaeol. Soc. 9* (n.s.) 26-43.

Morrison, I. (1969) An inexpensive photogrammetric approach to the reduction of survey diving time. *Underwater Assoc. Report 4,* 22-8.

——(1973a) Geomorphology and underwater observations of the Loch Awe area, in Hardy, ed. (1973).

——(1973b) Geomorphological investigation of marine and lacustrine environments of archaeological sites, using diving techniques. *Proc. 3rd Sci. Sympos. C.M.A.S.,* 41-6.

——(1976) (with Collings, L. & Farrell, R.) Earl Rognvald's Shipwreck: an investigation into Saga historicity. *Saga Book Vik. Soc. for Northern Research 19,* 2.3, 293-310.

——(1978a) Submerged stone circles in Loch Eye, Easter Ross. *Naut. Archaeol. Trust News* 1978.3.

——(1978b) Operational problems in the photographic recording of underwater archaeological sites. *Roy. Phot. Soc. Archaeol. Group J. Archaeolog 5,* 3-5.

——(1978c) A problematic 17th century duelling practice in Scotland. *Northern Studies 12,* 22-24.

——(1980a) Lake dwellings in the landscape, in Muckelroy, ed. (1980) 156-61.

——(1980b) Three experiments with shallow water survey techniques. *Naut. Archaeol. Trust News* 1980.3.

——(1981a) The extension of the chronology of the crannogs of Scotland. *IJNA 10.4,* 344-6.

——(1981b) The crannog off Ederline, Loch Awe, Argyll. *IJNA 10.4,* 347-9.

——(1981c) 'Hieland gallayis', Scots and Scandinavian traditions. *IJNA 10.4,* 275-6.

——(1982) An application of sonar controlled diving to the history of technology in Scotland. *Proc. 12th Conf. Underwater Archaeol.* New Orleans.

——(1983) Prehistoric Scotland, in Whittington & Whyte, eds. (1983) pp.1-24.

Muckleroy, K., ed. (1980) *Archaeology under Water – an Atlas of the World's Submerged Sites*. New York & London.

Munro, R. (1882) *Ancient Scottish Lake Dwellings or Crannogs*. Edinburgh.

——(1890) *The Lake-Dwellings of Europe*. London.

——(1893) Notes of crannogs or lake-dwellings recently discovered in Argyllshire. *PSAS 27*, 205-22.

——(1899) *Prehistoric Scotland*. Edinburgh.

——(1905) *Archaeology and False Antiquities*. London.

Murray, J. & Pullar, L. (1910) *Bathymetrical survey of the Scottish freshwater lochs*, 6 vols. Edinburgh.

Norton, W. (1984) *Historical Analysis in Geography*. London.

Oakley, G. (1973) *Scottish Crannogs*. Unpubl. M Phil thesis, Univ. of Newcastle.

Ottaway, B., ed. (1983) *Archaeology, Dendrochronology and the Radiocarbon Calibration Curve*. Univ. of Edinburgh Dept. Archaeol. Occas. Paper 9.

Oxford (1971) *The Oxford English Dictionary*. Oxford.

Pauli, L. (1984) *The Alps: Archaeology and Early History*. London.

Perini, R. (1976) Die Pfahlbauten im Torfmoor von Fiave. *Mit. der Schweiz. Gesellschaft für Ur- und Frühgesch. 27*, 2-12.

Piggott, C. M. (1952-53) Milton Loch Crannog I. A native house of the 2nd century A D in Kirkcudbrightshire. *PSAS 87*, 134-52.

Piggott, S. (1958) *Scotland before History*. London.

—— & Ritchie, G. (1982) *Scotland before History: with Gazetteer of Ancient Monuments*. Edinburgh.

Pryor, F. (1983) Down the drain, or how we discovered a Bronze Age 'crannog' at Flag Fen (Cambridgeshire). *Current Archaeol. 8*, 102-6.

Rankine, R. (1958) Oran na Comhachaig – Text and Tradition. *Trans. Gaelic Soc. Glasgow 5*, 122-71.

Reeves-Smyth, T. & Hamond, F., eds (1983) Landscape Archaeology in Ireland. *BAR 116*.

Renfrew, C. (1973) *Before Civilisation*. London.

——(1979) *Investigations in Orkney*. London.

Renfrew, C. & Cooke, K., eds (1979) *Transformations: Mathematical Approaches to Culture Change*. New York.

Renfrew, C. & Level, E. (1979) Predicting centres from polities, in Renfrew and Cooke, eds (1979).

Riddell, J. (1979) *Clyde Navigation: a history of the development and deepening of the River Clyde*. Edinburgh.

Ritchie, A. & G. (1981) *Scotland: Archaeology and Early History*. London.

Ritchie, J. (1942) The lake-dwelling or crannog in Eadarloch, Loch Treig: its traditions and its construction. *PSAS 76*, 8-78.

Rivet, A. L., ed. (1966) *The Iron Age in Northern Britain*. Edinburgh.

RCAHMS (1975) *Argyll Volume 2: Lorn*. Edinburgh.

Ruoff, U. (1981) Zürcher Seefersiedlungen. Von der Pfahlbauromantik zur modernen archäologischen Forschung. *Helvetia archaeologica 45-48*.

Rykwert, J. (1981) *On Adam's House in Paradise*. M.I.T. Press.

Rynne, E. & MacEoin, G. (1978) The Craggaunowen Crannog: Gangway and Gate Tower. *North Munster Antiquarian J. 20*, 47-56.

Salim, S. (1962) *Marsh Dwellers of the Euphrates Delta*. London.

Savory, L. (1973) *Aspects of Crannogs of the Solway–Clyde province*. Unpubl. MA Dissertation, Dept of Archaeology, Univ. of Edinburgh.

Schmid, P. (1978) New archaeological results of settlement structures in the NW German coastal area, in Cunliffe and Rowley, eds (1978) pp.123-45.

Scott, J. G. (1960) Loch Glashan. *Discovery & Excavation*, 8-9.

Selinge, K-G. (1979) *Agrarian Settlements and Hunting Grounds*. Stockholm.

Shotton, F., ed. (1977) *British Quaternary Studies: Recent Advances*. Oxford.

Smout, C. (1969) *History of the Scottish People*. London.

Speck, J. (1981) Pfahlbauten: Dichtung oder Wahrzeit? *Helvetia archaeologica 45-48*, 98-138.

Steer, K. & Bannerman, J. (1977) *Late Medieval Monumental Sculpture in the West Highlands*. RCAHMS.

Stevenson, J. (1975) Survival and Discovery, in Evans, Limbrey & Cleere, eds (1975) pp.104-9.

Stevenson, R. (1966) Metalwork and some other objects in Scotland and their cultural affinities, in Rivet, ed. (1966) pp.17-44.

Stewart, M. (1969) The Ring Forts of Central Perthshire. *Trans. and Proc. Perthshire Soc. Nat. Sci. for 1965-68, 12,* 21-32.

Strahm, C. (1976) Deux stations lacustres sur le lac de Neuchâtel. *Archeologia 99,* 55-71.

Stuart, J. (1864-66) Notices of a group of artificial islands in the Loch of Dowalton, Wigtonshire, and of other artificial islands or 'crannogs' throughout Scotland. *PSAS 6,* 114-78.

——(1866) Notice of the Scotch Crannogs, in Keller (1866) pp.389-92.

Thesiger, W. (1964) *The Marsh Arabs.* London.

Tuan, Yi-Fu (1979) *Landscapes of Fear.* Oxford.

Watkins, T. (1980) A prehistoric coracle in Fife. *IJNA 9.4,* 277-86.

Welch, A. (1978) *Accidents Happen.* London.

Whittington, G. & Whyte, I., eds (1983) *An Historical Geography of Scotland.* New York.

Williams, J. (1971) A crannog at Loch Arthur, New Abbey. *Trans. Dumfries & Galloway N. H. & A. Soc. 58,* 106-20.

Wood-Martin, W. (1886) *The Lake Dwellings of Ireland: commonly called Crannogs.* Dublin.

Young, G. & Wheeler, N. (1977) *Return to the Marshes.* London.

Placename and Site Index

The letter f indicates a reference to a figure on that page

111

General Index

The letter f indicates a reference to a figure on that page

access to crannogs (see also gangways,
  causeways, boats, jetties, docks),
  21-2, 54-7, 59, 74
aggressive use of crannogs, 23-4, 28-9, 64-5
A'Chomhachag (The Houlet's Sang), 67
agriculture and crannogs, 21, 53, 64, 70-80
Ailean na Leine Ruaidhe (Allan Red
  Sark), 4
air reconnaissance, 85, plates 1, 4, 5, 6, 8, 9
Alexander I, King, 4
Antonine Wall, 69f, 70
ards and ploughs, 8, 24, 70, 71f
atlas of surveyed sites, 31f-37f

ballast mounds, 17
Bartlett, R. (cartographer), 51-2
bathymetrical survey, 2, 60, 84-5
black house, 55f
Blaeu maps, 29f
Blundell, O., vii, 4-6, 8, 44, 81, 84, 102
boats, 21, 39, 56f, 57, 59, 67, 69f
breakwaters, 31f, 54, 55f, 64, 88,
  plate 18

cartographic evidence, 29f, 30, 51, 52f,
  77-8, 79f
'causeways', 31f, 32f, 45f, 54, 69f, 87
chevaux de frise, 51
Childe, V. G., 12, 59-60
chronology of crannogs
  general problems, 58, 72
  date range, 1, 6, 9, 12, 22-5, 40
  dated sites: Eadarloch, 6
    Milton Loch I, 6, 8, 24
    L. Tay: Fearnan H., 24; Firbush, 24;
      Oakbank, 24
    L. Awe: Ederline, 24

radiocarbon conventions, ix; limitations
  24-5, 49
dendrochronology: potential, 12, 49, 93
typological problems, 12, 20
documentary evidence, 6, 22-4
multi-period sites, 6, 12-13
circular crannog huts, 21, 54
circular mound structures (see also radial),
  39, 43f, 45f
classification of built-up islets, 12-13,
  16-20, 26
computers
  Apple with Robotics interactive
    graphics, ix, 92
  computer-aided graphics, 31f-35f, 47f,
    48f, 50f, 55f, 63f, 65f, 76f, 89f, 92, 95f
  database potential, 92-3
construction techniques, 20-21, 28-9,
  37-57, 86-7
continuum, artificial and natural islets,
  19-20, 37-38, 72, 86, 100
Cregeen, E., 8
Cumming (Comyn), Lord, 27-9, 53-4, 65

dates *see* chronology of crannogs
deceptive sites, 17-18
demolition of crannogs, 23-4, 84
dimensions of crannogs
  conventions, ix
  height of structures, 61, 75
  plan comparisons: between crannogs,
    31f-36f; with other site types, 37f, 55f,
    75, 76f
Dio Cassius, 1
distance offshore, 61, 64, 65f
diving, viii, 4-6, 8-9, 10f, 17, 27, 38, 50,
  81-96, 100, 102

115

Dixon, T. N., viii-x, 9, 92-3, 96, plate 10
'docks', 17f, 18f, 31f, 33f, 36f, 37f, 50f, 54, 55f, 64, 69f, 89f
documentary evidence, 1, 6, 14, 17-18, 22-4, 28-30, 65-7, 72, 77-8, 99
drainage of sites, vii, 2, 12, 16, 83
dredging, 19
droving, 68
duns and relationship to crannogs, 25, 37f, 63f, 65f, 75, 76f, 100

Edgerton, H., x, 85, 88, plates 18, 19
estuarine sites, 8, 16-17, 60
ethnographic parallels, 1-2, 3f, 4, 15f, 66, 72, 99
etymology 25-7, 52-3
excavation
    deficiencies of early digs, 6, 8, 20, 44-5, 46f, 58, plate 13
    modern underwater excavation, 92-6, plates 7, 10, 14, 16, 17, 22, 24
exposure see storm-wave attack

Farquharson's survey (L.Tay 1769), 78, 79f
feasting-houses, 66-7
field systems, 77-8, 79f
fishing and fowling, 22, 64, 67, 85, 94f
flax-retting pounds, 17
foundations, 20, 37-8, 40-2, 53, 61-2, 75, 78
functions see reasons for building or using crannogs
gangways, 7f, 15f, 17f, 18f, 22, 35f, 36f, 37f, 41f, 49f, 50f, 54, 65f, 87
gatehouse, 54
geographical determinism, 57, 59
geographical distribution
    misconceptions, 12
    problems of analysis, 8-9, 10f, 58-60, 71-2, 75-7, 83-5, 99-101
    implications of distributions, 40, 72, 74-8, 79f, 100-1

history of research, 4-15
homesteads, 8, 21, 70, 74, 76-7
hunting-lodges, 66-7

identification of crannogs, 39, 86-7
island duns, 37

'jetties', 32f, 33f, 54, 64
joist construction, 27-9, 53f, 54

Keller, F., 5, 14, 15f, 23
kelpies, 4

lake-dwellings, 8, 21, 70, 74
lake-level changes, 13, 19, 40, 84
lake-side settlements, 13, 15f, 16, 19, 84
lake-village hypothesis, 72, 73f, 74
landscape
    topography and physical evolution, 2, 19, 38-40, 60-2, 72, 74-5, 84
    cultural relations, organisation, 1, 4, 13, 57, 64-80, 84, 100
La Tène brooch, 69f, 70
loch numbers and sizes, 2, 62, 85

McArdle, D., viii, x, 8, 9,
Macbeth, 4
Mackintosh clan, 23-4, 57, 65, 68
managed woodlands, 97
Maoris, 99
Mapleton, R., 6, 44
marine sites, 8, 17, 60
Marsh-Arab island villages, 3f, 4
mortice joints, 44
Munro, R., vif, vii-viii, 6, 20-1, 38, 42, 43f, 44, 66, 68-70, 81, 83, 96, 99, 102
Murray, F., 8
Murray, Sir J., 2, 60, 84-85

Naval Air Command, 9
non-disturbance surveys, 20, 46, 83, 86, 101

Oakley, G., 8
oral traditions, 1, 4, 14, 66-8, 72
organic material
    differential survival, 14, 41-2, 77, 92-3, 95-6, 101, plates 7, 10, 11, 12, 14, 15, 16, 17
    conservation problems, 95-97, 101
Owl of Strone see A'Chomhachag

Perspektomat graphics, ix, 92
Pfahlbauromantik, 5, 13
photography underwater, 91-2, plates 7, 10, 14, 16, 17, 22, 24

116

Piggott, C. M. (Guido), 6, 20, 48, 49f
Piggott, S., 8, 58
pile-dwellings, 5, 13, 16, 50
piles and pile driving, 39-40, 42, 50, 51f, 61, 87
place-name evidence, 1, 26-7
ploughs and ards, 8, 24, 70, 71f
pollarding, 97
Pont, T. (cartographer), 29f
Prince Regent (dredger), 19
prison islands, 66

radial mound structures (see also circular), 45f, 46
reasons for building or using crannogs, 1, 4, 19, 21-2, 24, 53, 64-80
rectangular crannog huts, 21, 54, 55f
rectangular mound structures, 39, 44f, 46, 47f
Register, Privy Council of Scotland, 23
research strategy, 8-9, 30, 58, 70-1, 81-98
'ring forts', 37f, 76-7, 79f
Ritchie, J., 6, 46, 47f, 48f, 51f, 67
river sites, 17, 60
Romans, 1-2, 6, 12, 49, 69f, 70
roof reconstruction, 49
routeways, 57-59, 68, 69f, 70
Roy, W. (military survey), 2
Ruoff, U., 5, 9, 13-14, 91, 93

Savory, L., 8
search techniques, 83-85, plates 5, 6, 8, 9
security, 1-2, 21, 37f, 50f, 51-3, 64-6
shelter *see* storm wave attack
sheilings, 68, 78, 79f

sonar, 17, 85, 88, plates 18, 19
Stalcair Rioch (Brindled Stalker), 4
stereotypes of crannogs, 16, 17f, 18f, 19, 45-6, 47f, 48, 49f, plates 2, 3, 23
'stone crannogs', 20, 37-40, 62
storm-wave attack, 41, 60, 62, 63f, 64, 73f, 75
Stuart, J., 1, 5
submergence (subsidence, compaction), 40-2, 61-2
see also lake-level changes
surveying techniques
site morphology, 87-8, 89f, 90f, plates 6, 8, 20, 21
excavation recording, 89-92, 91f, 95f

Telford, T., 19
Terp settlement, 3f
tool-marks, 96-7, plates 7, 15
topography *see* landscape
transhumance, 66, 78
treenails, 44
Turks, 42

'used wood', 97

vermin, 53f, 64
Vogt, E., 13

water depth, 61, 65f, 73f, 75
Weirde settlement, 3f
wetlands sites, 13, 16, 19
wickerwork, 52
Wood-Martin, W., viii, 28, 41
world distribution of built-up islets, 2, 3f, 13, 99

117